Mountain Bluebirds

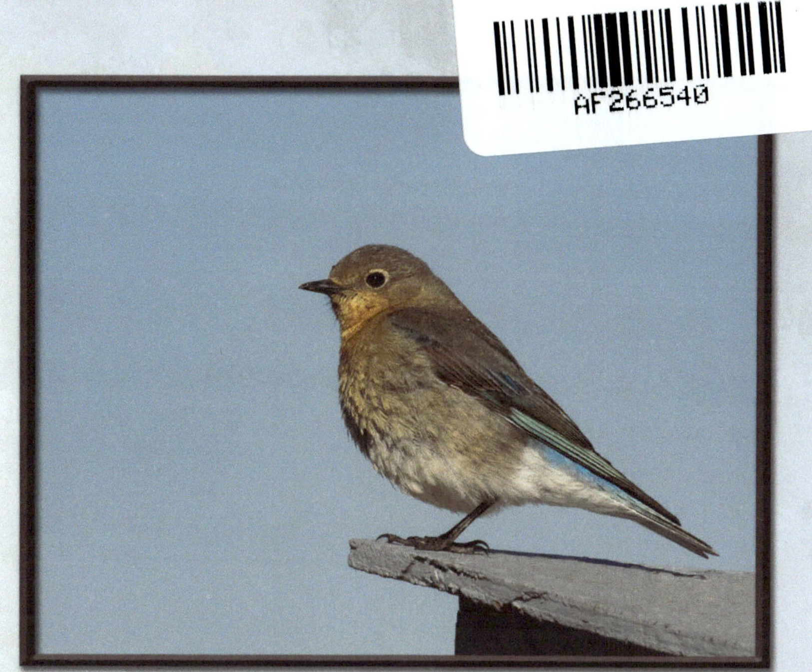

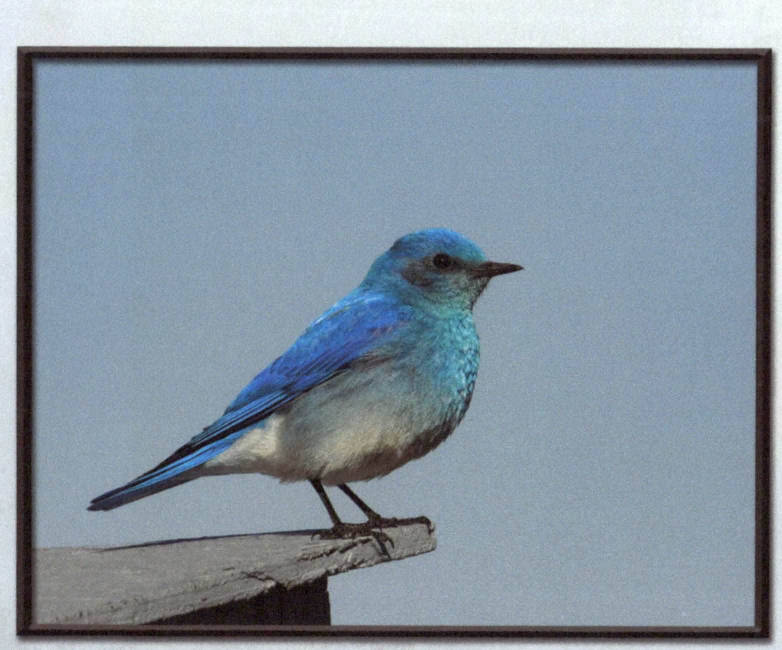

Lois Lake

In August of 2017 I discovered a lump in my breast. After many
tests and a biopsy, I was diagnosed with breast cancer. My
world was turned upside down with one simple phone call. Over
the next year, with the support of my family, I went through
twenty weeks of chemotherapy, surgery and six weeks of radiation;
five days a week. My life was consumed with treatments and
doctor appointments. I needed something to occupy my mind and
bring a sense of normalcy, even if for just a few hours of the day.
Photography is a passion that I enjoy but even more than that,
photography is a spiritual connection for me. When I am outside
taking photographs, I marvel at the beauty that God has created.
I am in awe of the birds and animals that He put on this earth. I
love observing their behavior.

God created us with the ability to make choices. I decided I was
not going to allow this cancer to take over my life. I chose to
enjoy my photography and the beauty that God has given us.
Most of the images in this book were taken while I was having
radiation treatments.

I would like to dedicate this book to all who are going through
a difficult time. Each one of us will have a time in our life when
we need someone bigger than we are to help us get through
that valley.

God loves you and will walk through
that difficult journey with you. God
has given us so much beauty and
love. All we need to do is choose
to accept it. As you are reading this
book, I pray God's love will pour
over you and give you strength and
peace and comfort.

We have two types of bluebirds in Colorado. The western bluebird (*Siala mexicana*) can be readily recognized by the red feathers on the male's breast.

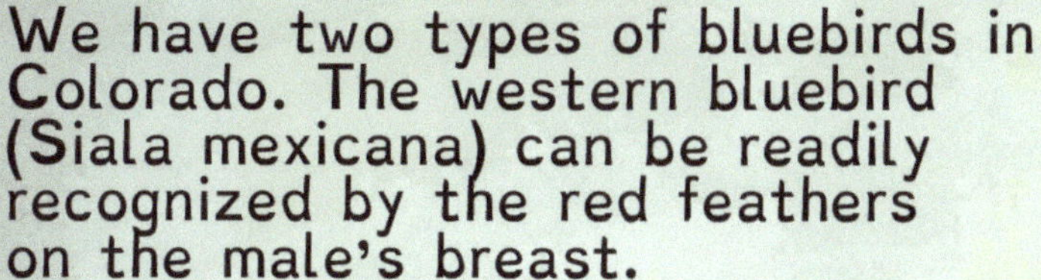

The mountain bluebird, (S. currucoides) on the other hand has white feathers on the male's breast. The female mountain bluebird is pale sky-blue with a light-colored chin, a brownish back and may have a rufous tint on her breast in early spring.

This book is about the mountain bluebird.

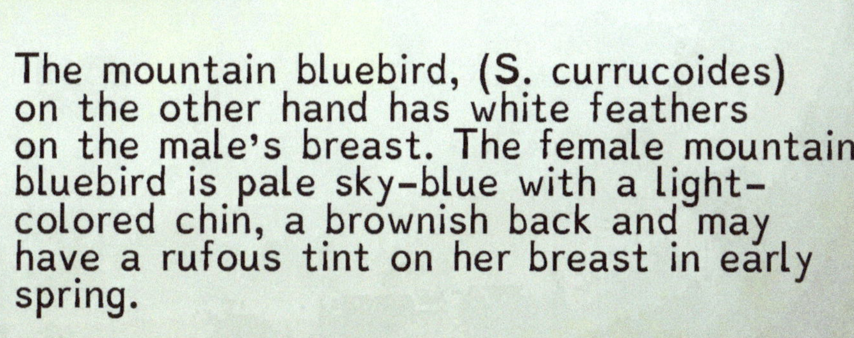

Bluebirds do not stay in Colorado year-round. They spend the winter in Mexico. Each spring I eagerly await the return of the bluebirds and make a note on my calendar. In 2018, I saw my first bluebird of the year on February 25. The trees were not yet budded out. Quite often we will have several more snow storms after the bluebirds arrive.

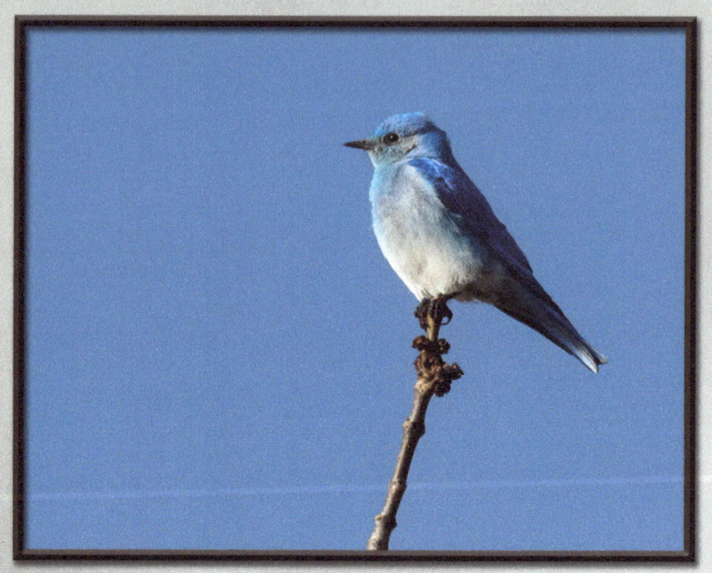

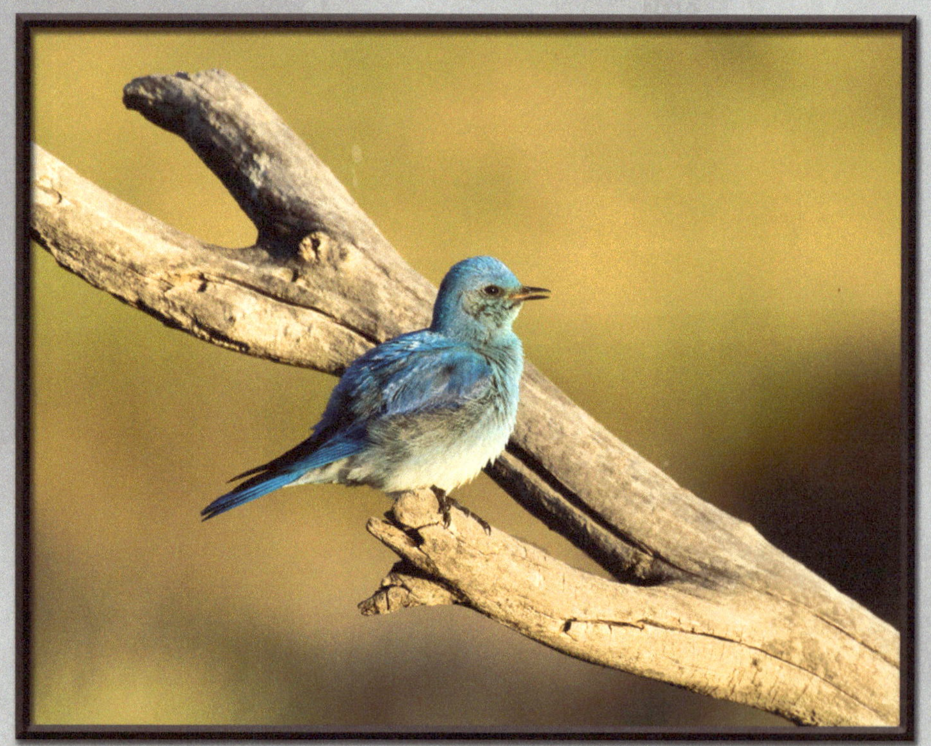

The temperatures still get into the thirties at night. The male perches on a branch with his feathers all fluffed up to get warm in the early morning light.

The male generally arrives
in the territory about two
weeks before we see the
female. He checks out the
surrounding area for food
and safety. He scouts out
possible nesting locations.

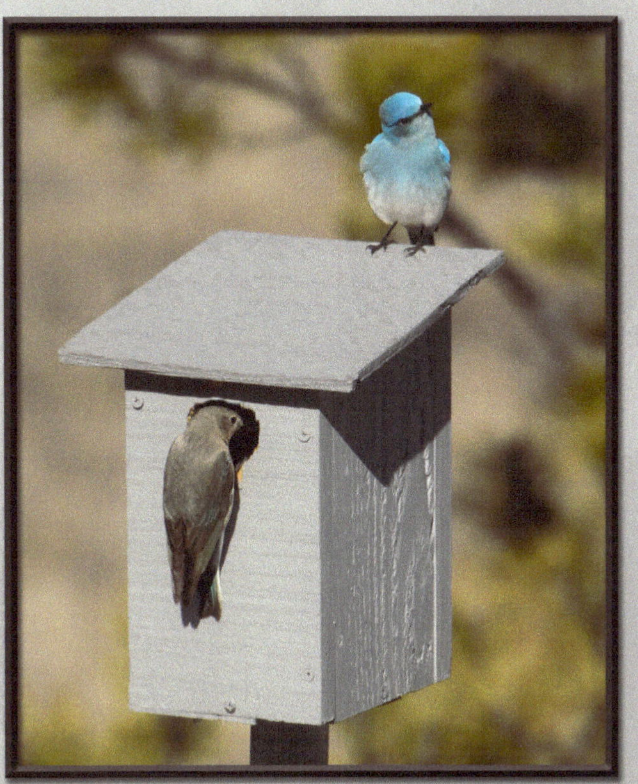

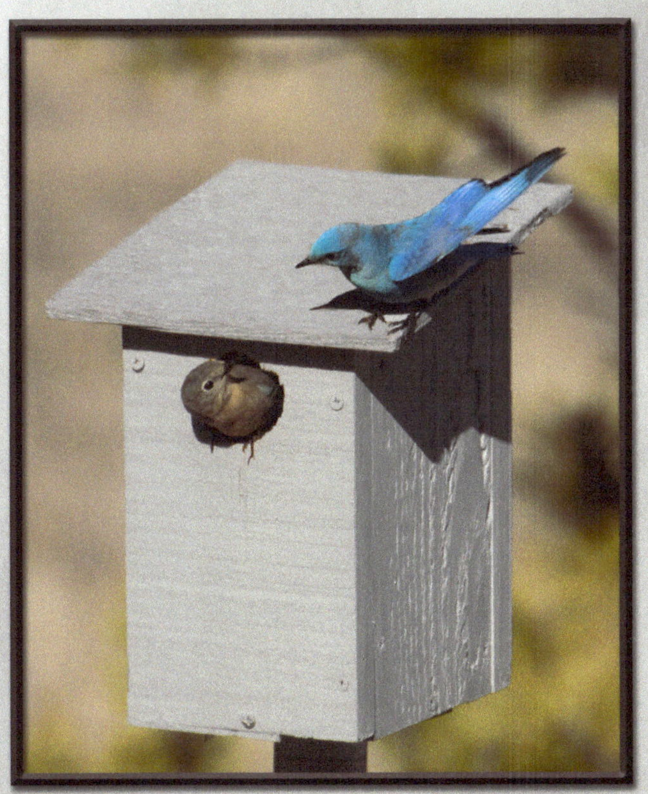

When he finds a place that he
feels is suitable for nesting,
he claims the territory and
starts defending it. The
female chooses the nest
she wants to use.

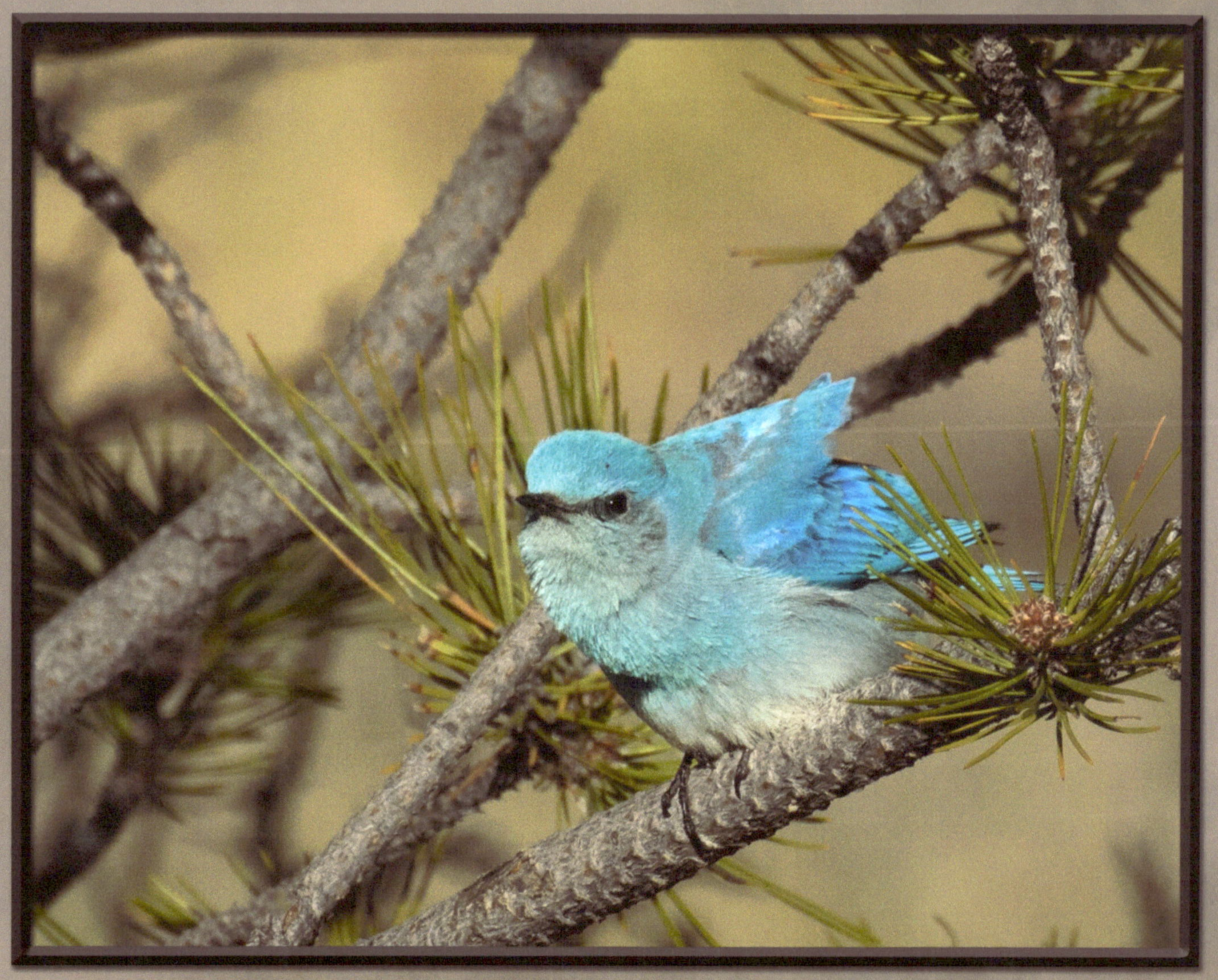

The courting male sings in a tree nearby the nest. He twitters, gets his feathers all fluffed up and flutters his wings as a demonstration to attract the female.

He flies back and forth between the nest and a perch near the female.

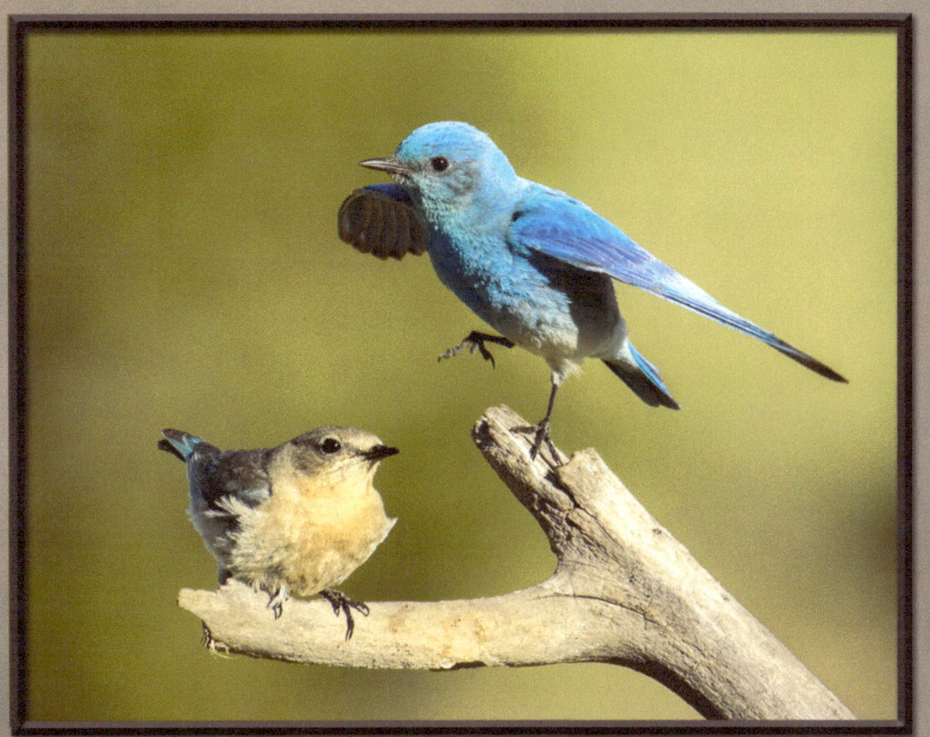

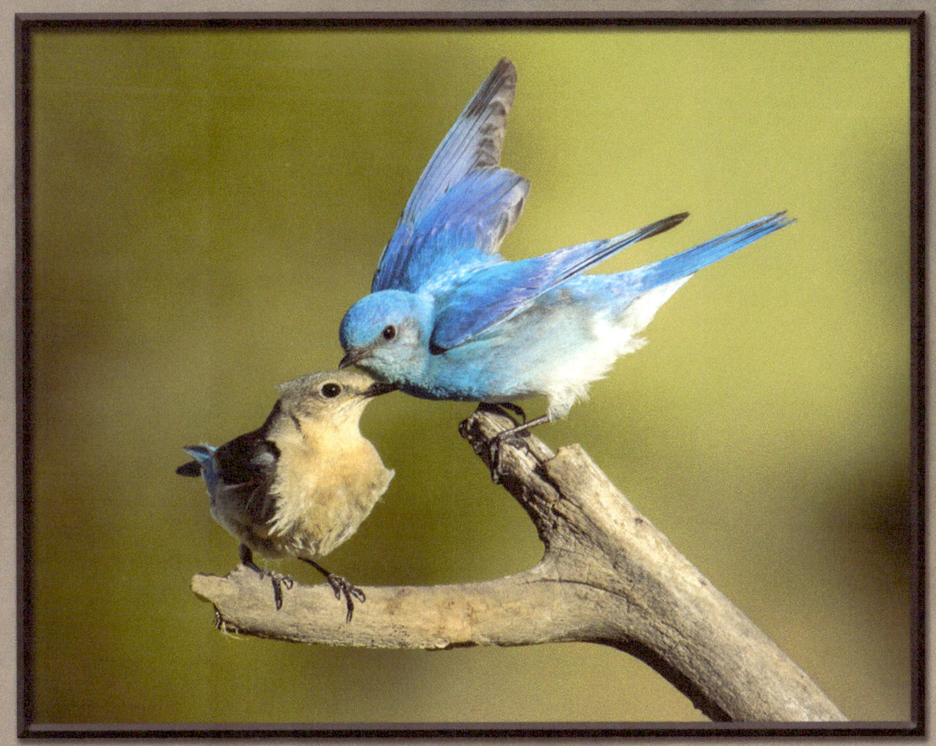

Once the nesting site is chosen, the bluebirds have much to discuss.

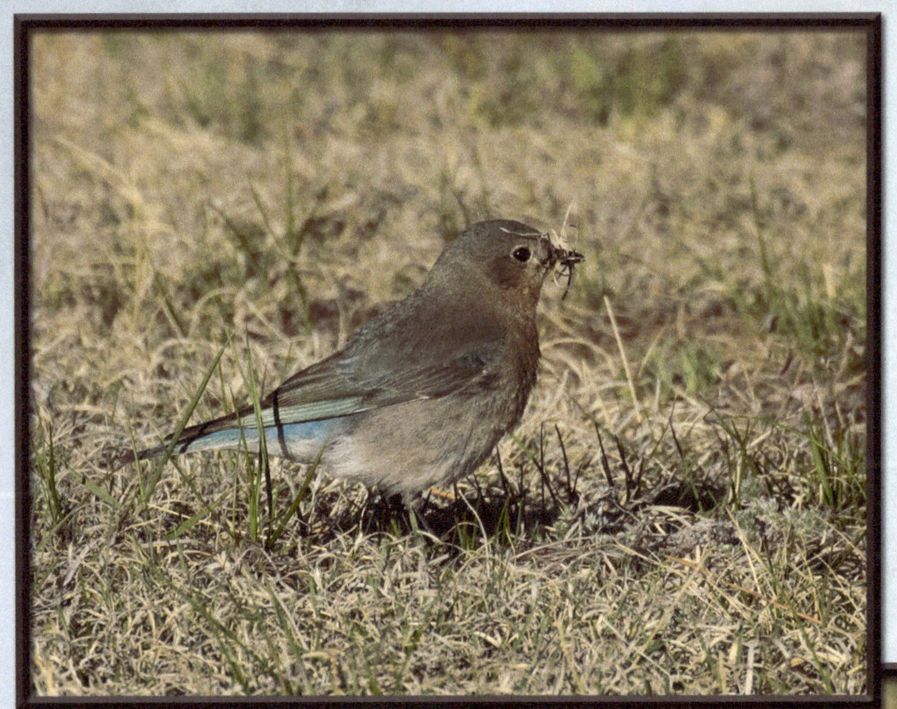

The female bluebird gathers dead grass to start building the nest.

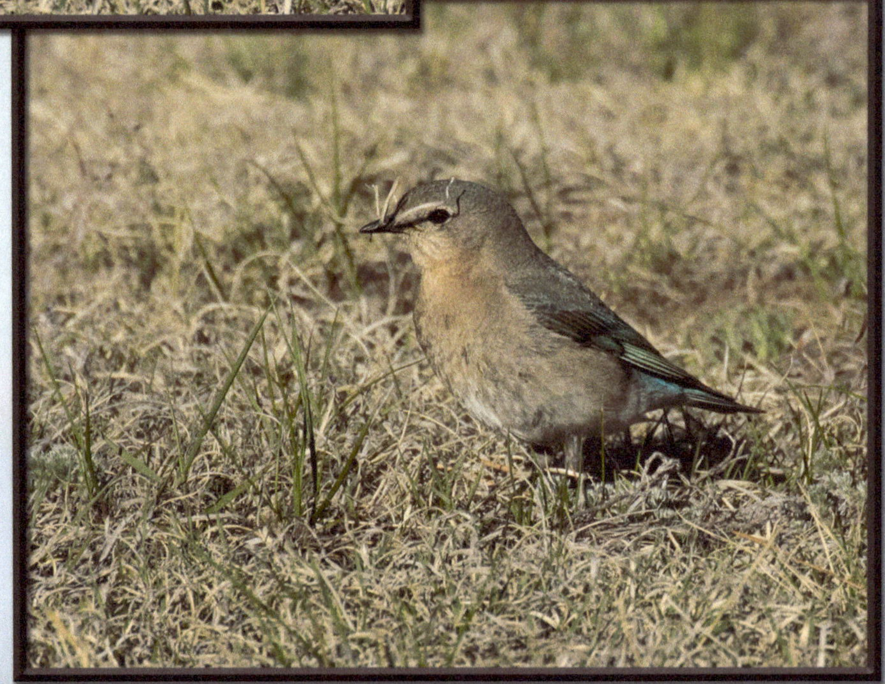

The male mountain bluebird also contributes to building the nest, especially during courtship. He perches on the branch looking below for just the right piece of grass.

The whole process of building a nest can take as long as a week. Most of the activity happens in the early morning.

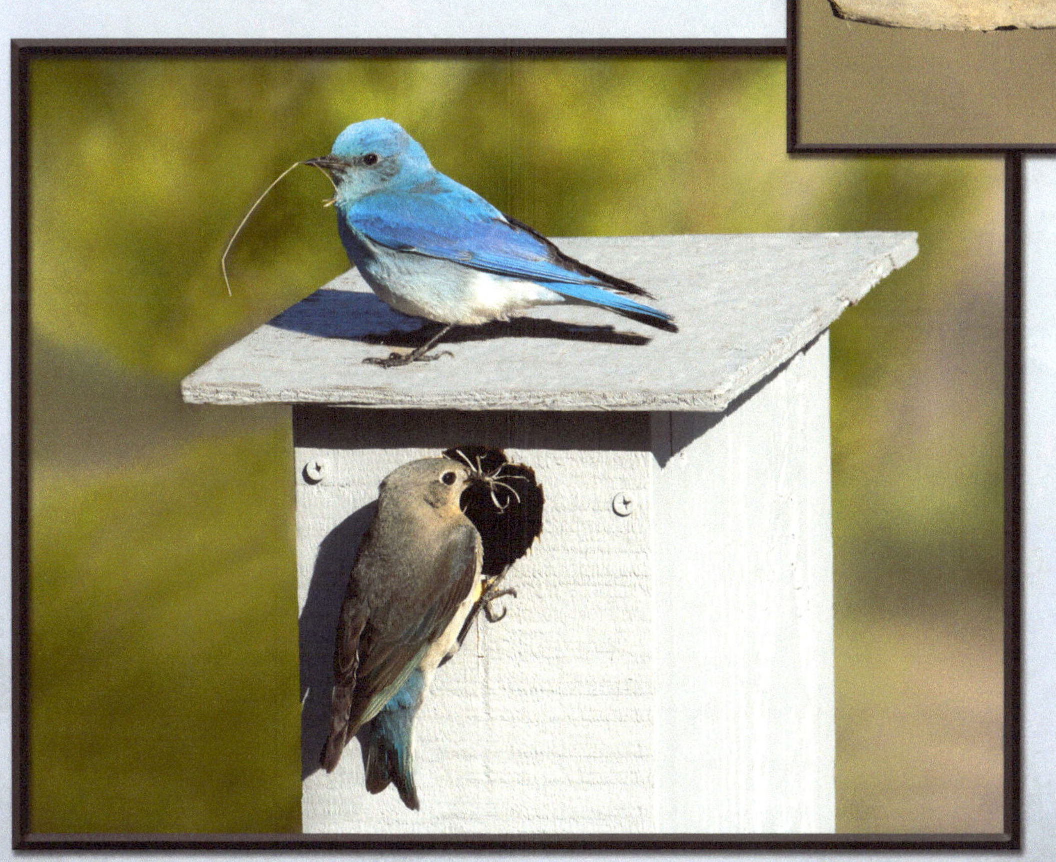

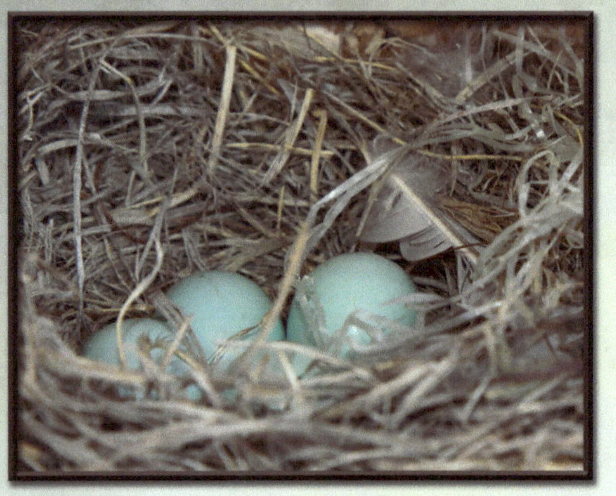

Bluebird nests are made of woven grass, straw and sometimes feathers. When the nest is finished, the female will lay one egg each day until the clutch is complete. The eggs are light blue and about the size of a large marble. They generally lay three to four eggs in each clutch. Incubation starts right after the last egg is laid and usually takes thirteen to fourteen days for the chicks to hatch.

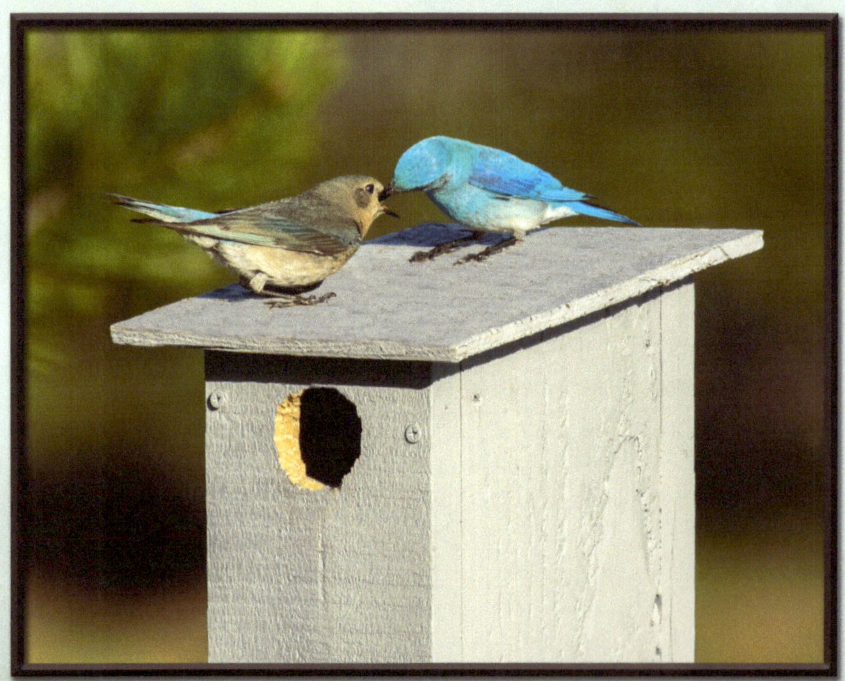

While the female incubates the eggs, the male brings food to her, so she does not have to leave the nest for any length of time.

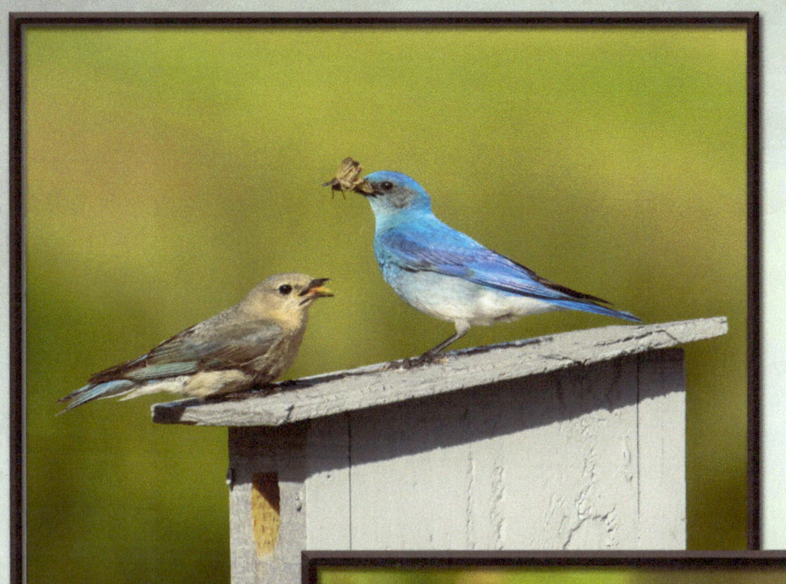

As the male approaches
with food, he chirps to
announce that he is
bringing food and the
female comes to the top
of the nesting box to
get it. She may beg,
fledgling-style with open
beak, quivering wings,
and begging calls.

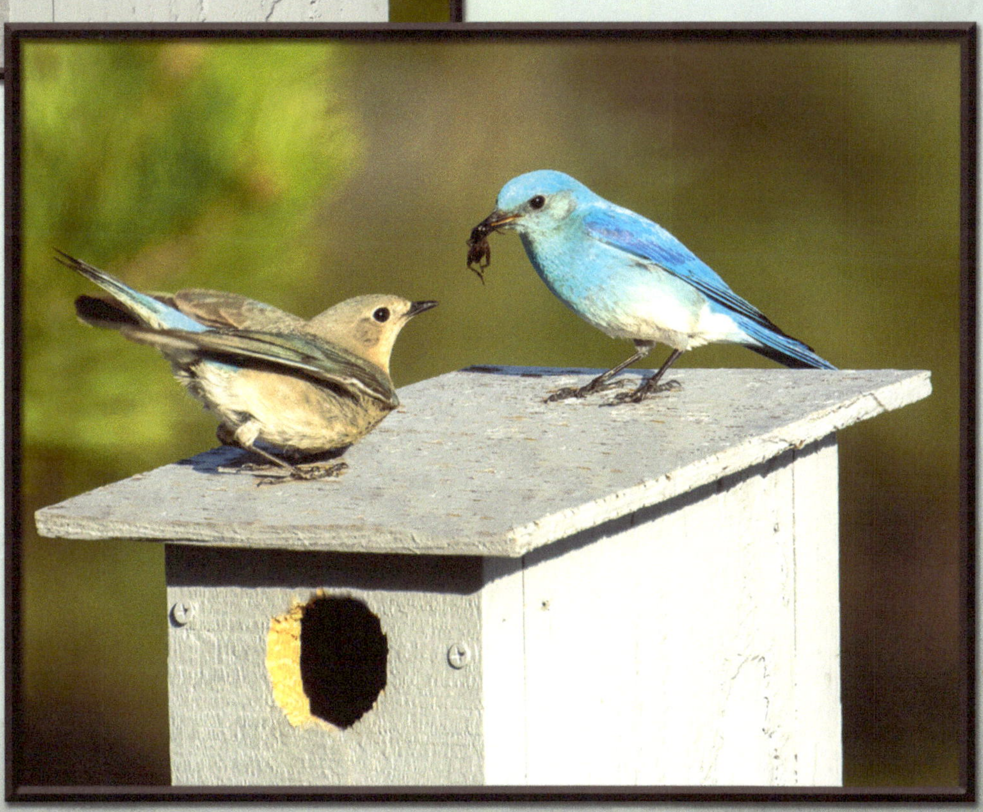

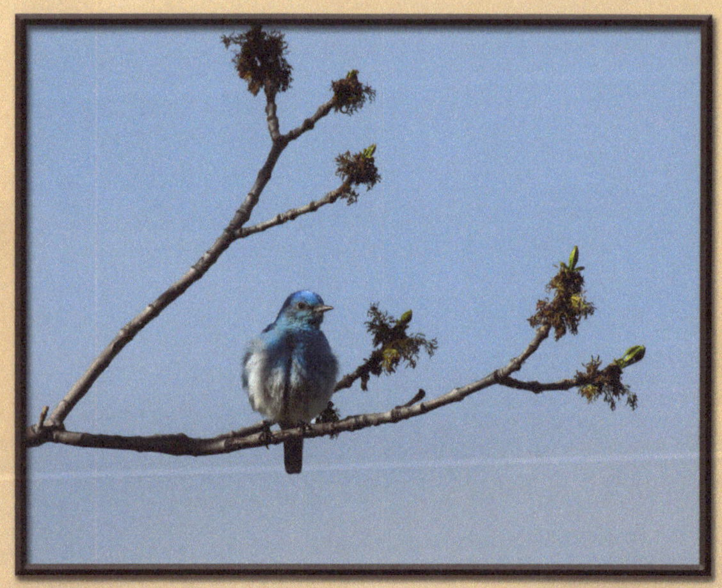

The leaves have not budded
out, so the male has a clear
view of the surrounding area.
He guards the nest while the
female incubates the eggs.
She sleeps in the nest during
incubation while the male
roosts nearby.

The babies are naked
when they hatch, and
their eyes are closed.
They are totally
helpless. By day three,
their ear opening is
evident. From the day
they hatch to about
day five, their digestive
system can only handle
soft-bodied insects
and larva.

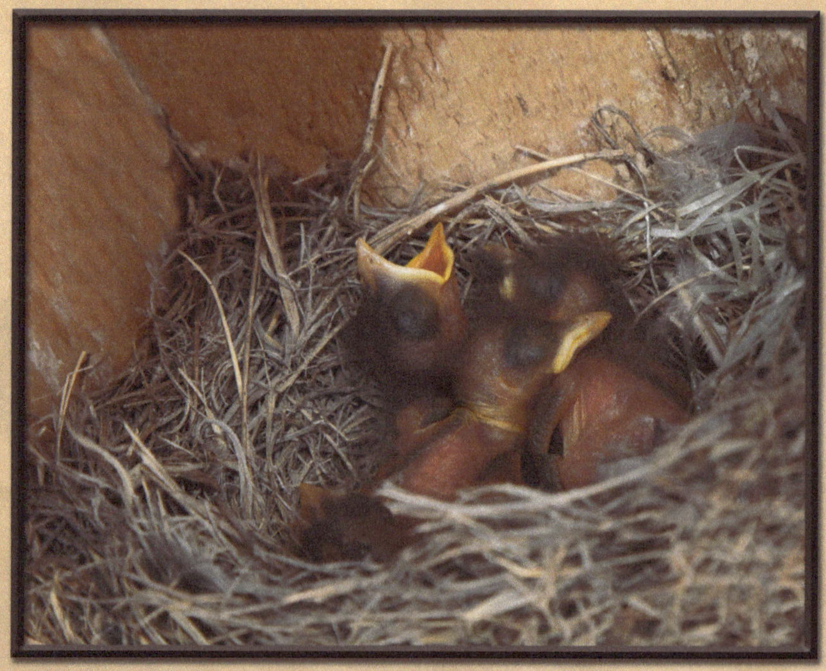

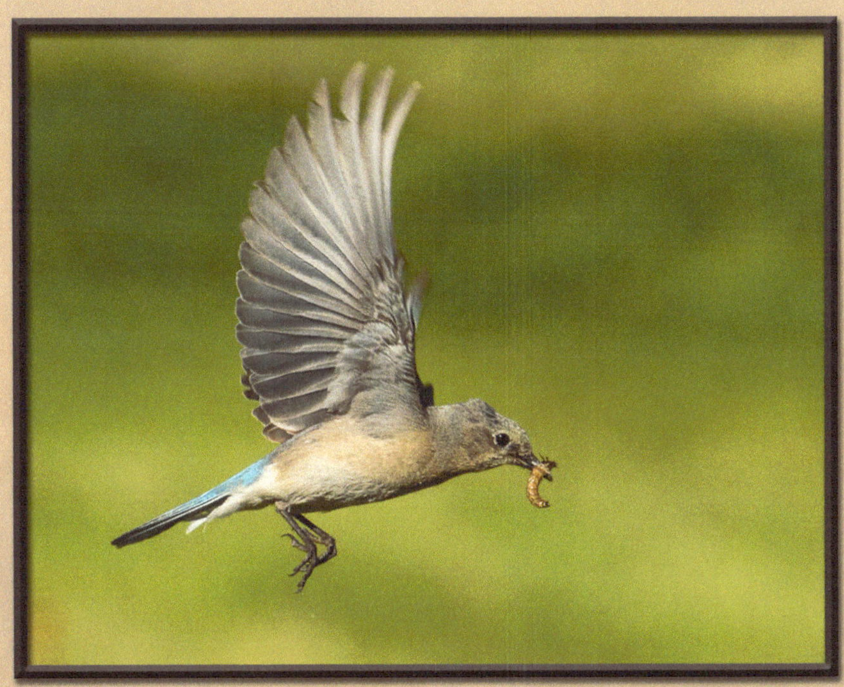

Mama brings in a
soft-bodied grub
worm.

The flying ants
are small and
easy for the
young chicks
to digest.

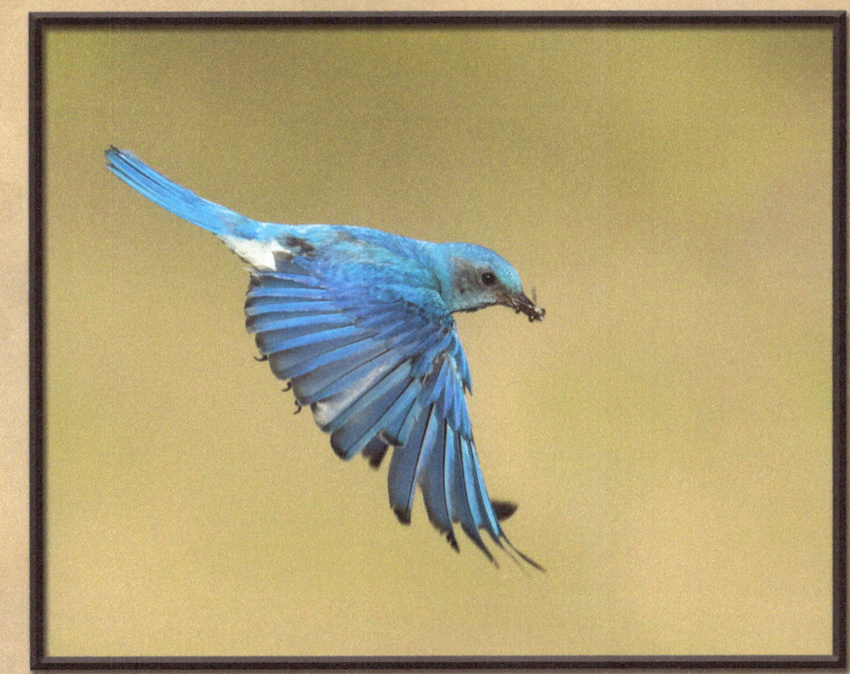

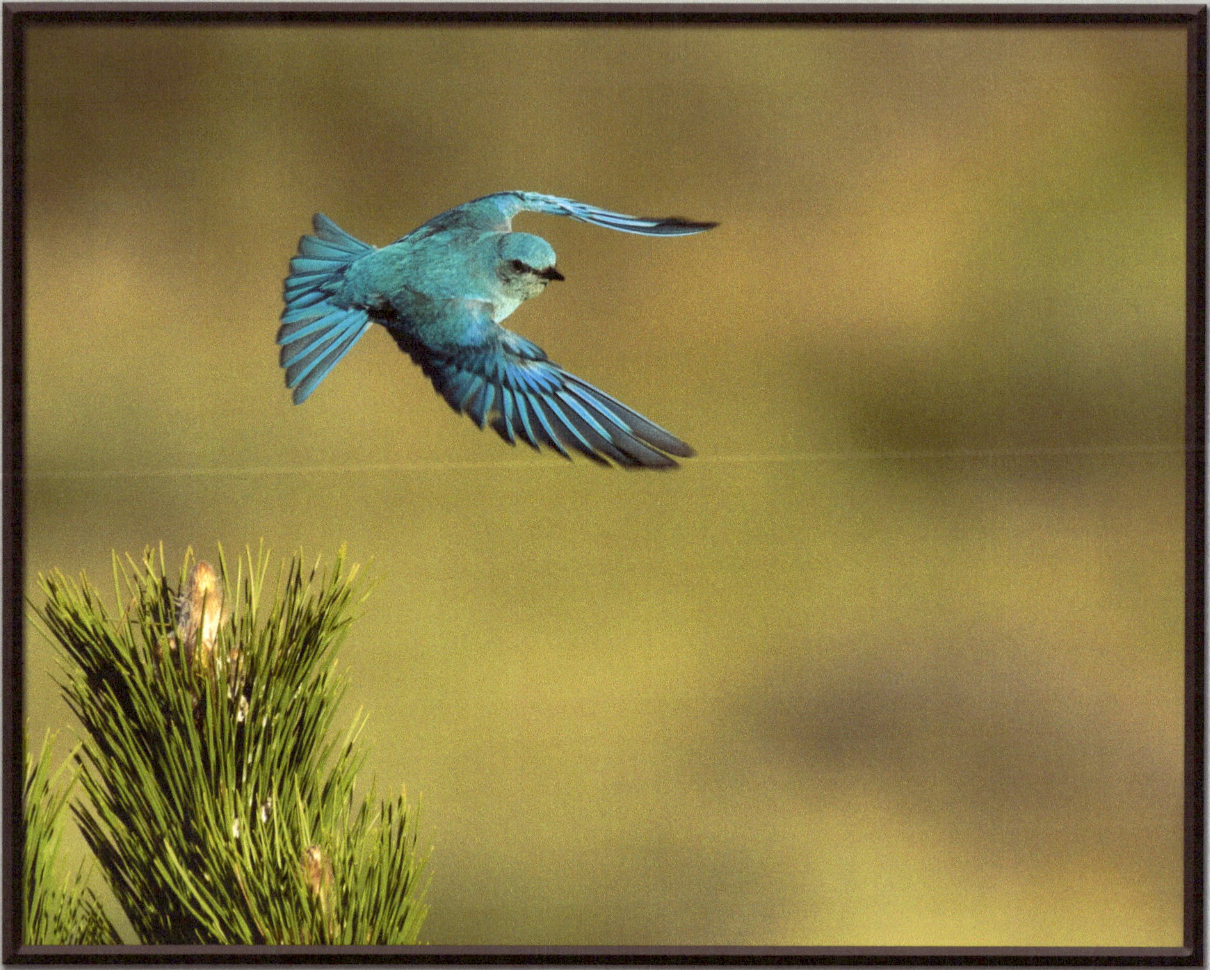

The male perched high in the top of
the pine tree waiting for a bug to
make a movement and reveal itself.
Shortly it paid off and he dived down
to get the bug.

They also hunt while in flight,
hovering before dropping onto the
prey, or snatching insects in the air.

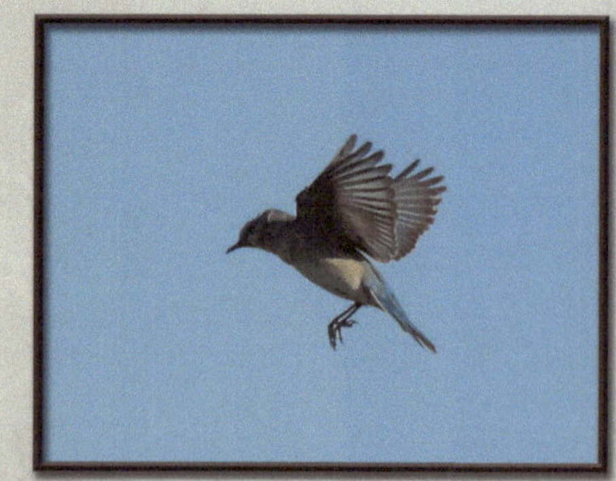

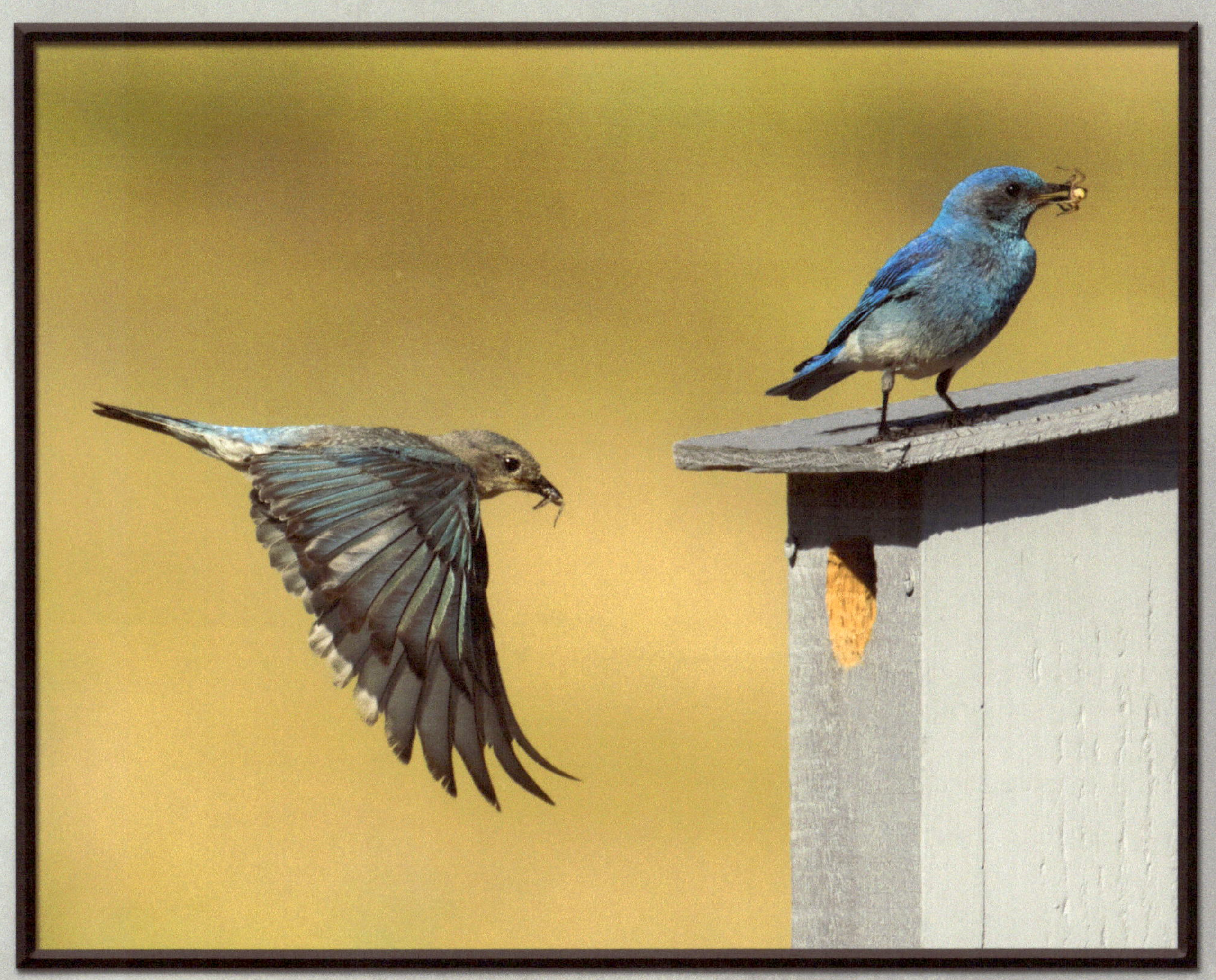

The chicks grow very fast and need a lot of food for that growth. The adults bring in food about every fifteen to twenty minutes.

The birds land
on top of the
nesting box and
look around for
any danger
before taking
the food in for
the chicks.

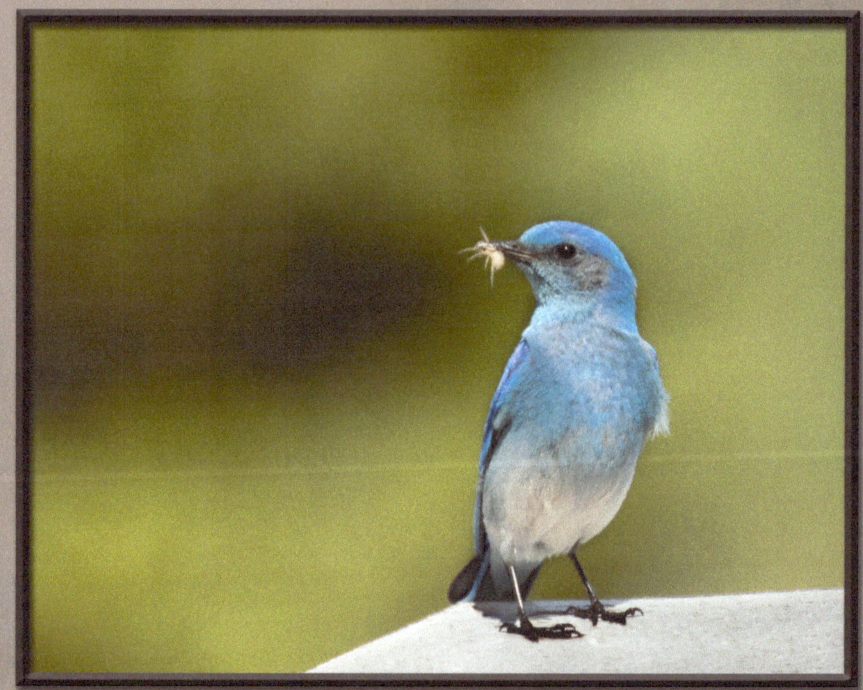

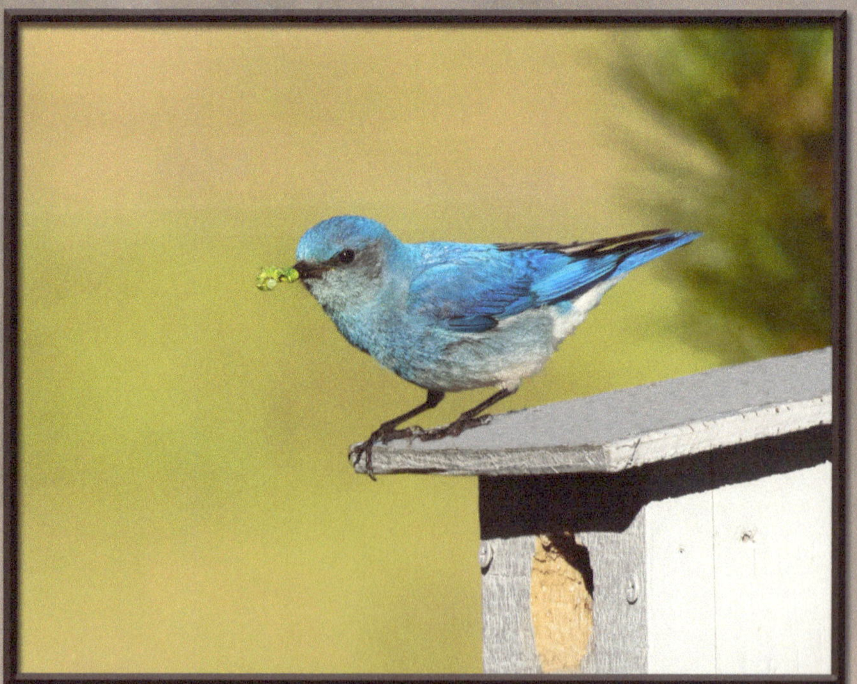

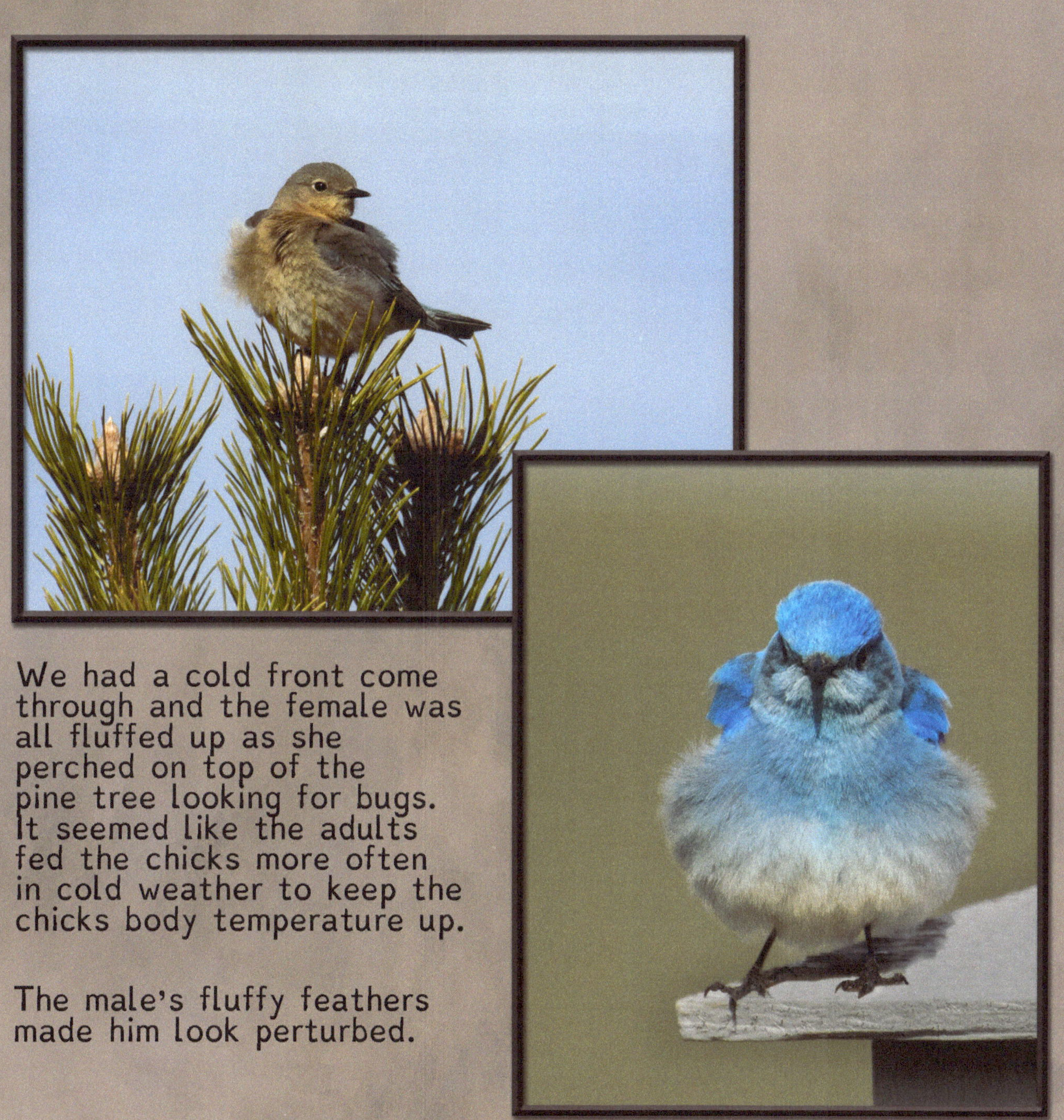

We had a cold front come
through and the female was
all fluffed up as she
perched on top of the
pine tree looking for bugs.
It seemed like the adults
fed the chicks more often
in cold weather to keep the
chicks body temperature up.

The male's fluffy feathers
made him look perturbed.

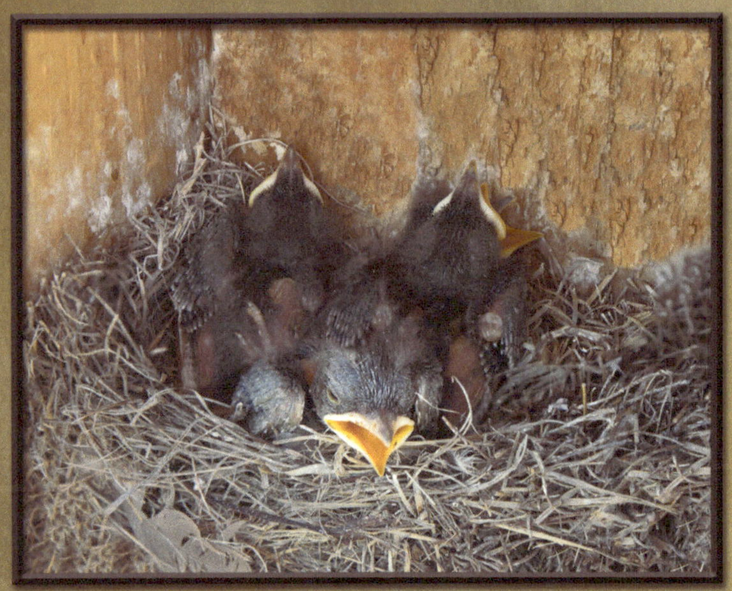

Between day five and day eight after hatching, you can begin to see their feathers developing and their eyes open.

Five days after hatching, the baby's digestive system can handle grasshoppers and hard-bodied insects.

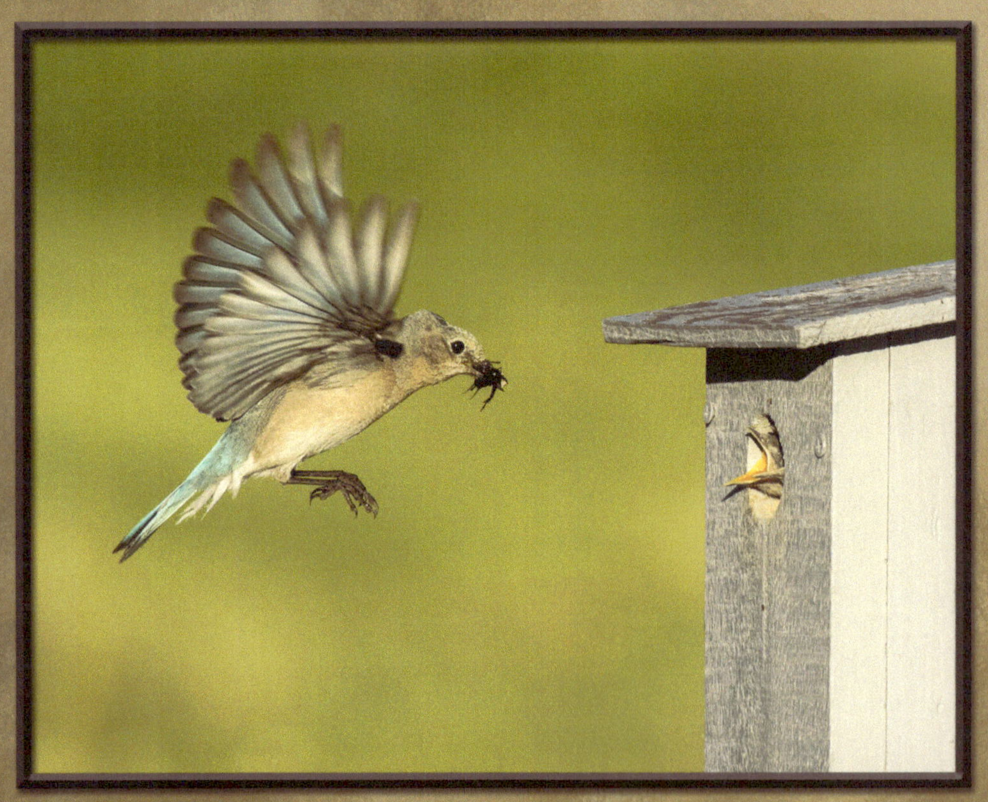

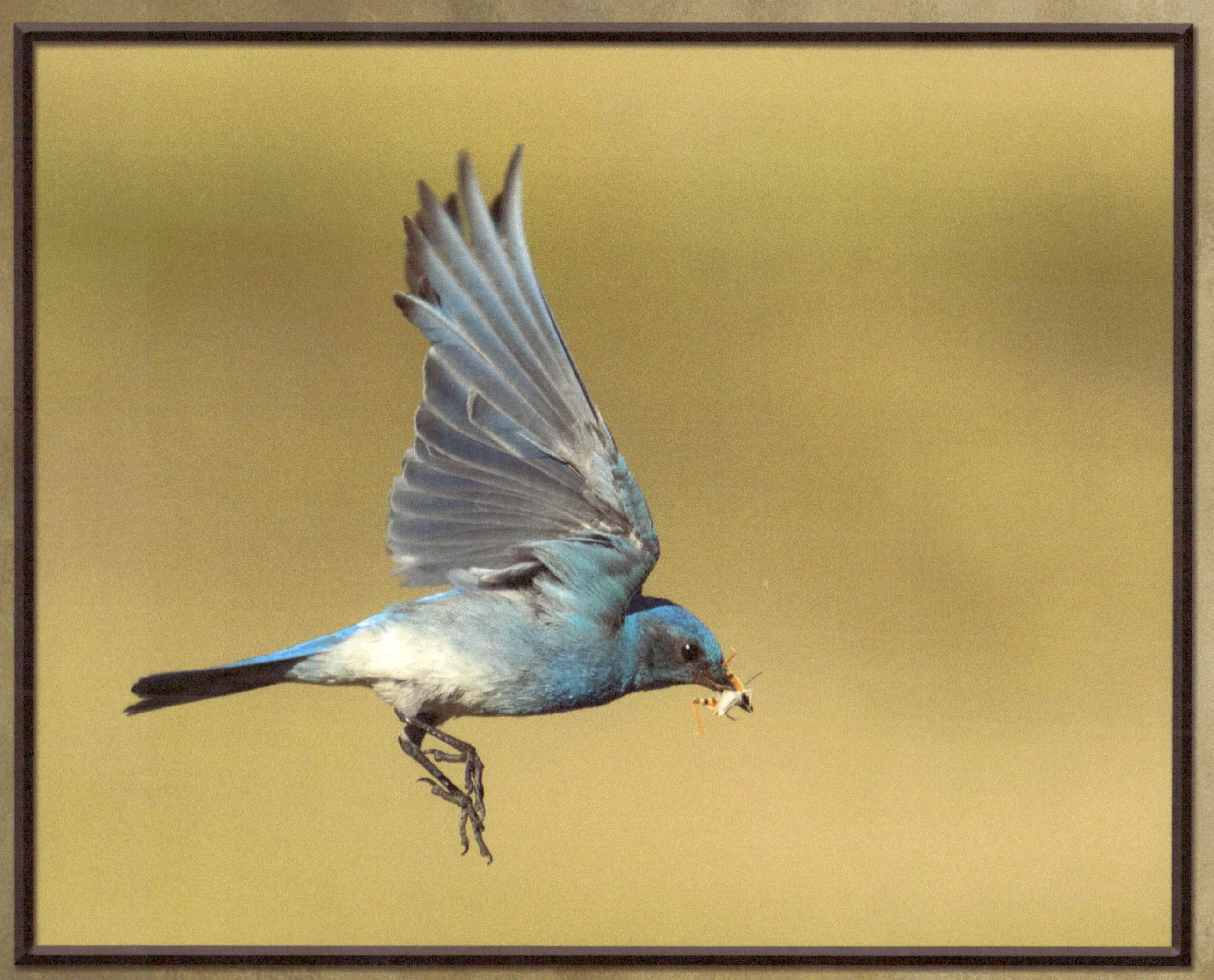

Daddy brings a grasshopper to the nest.

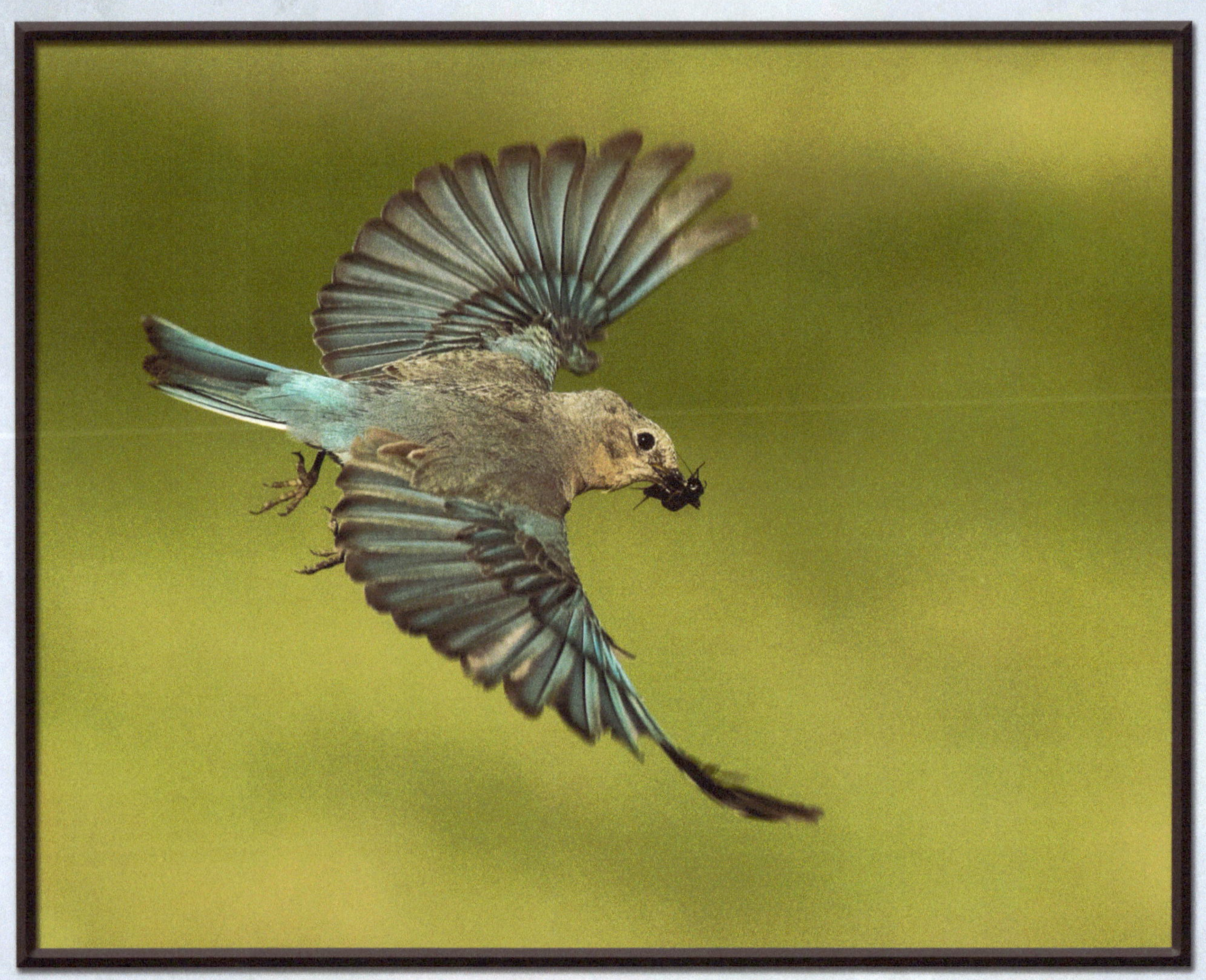

Grasshoppers and crickets seem to be abundant and a main source of food. It is a good thing because there are four hungry chicks chirping, "feed me, feed me."

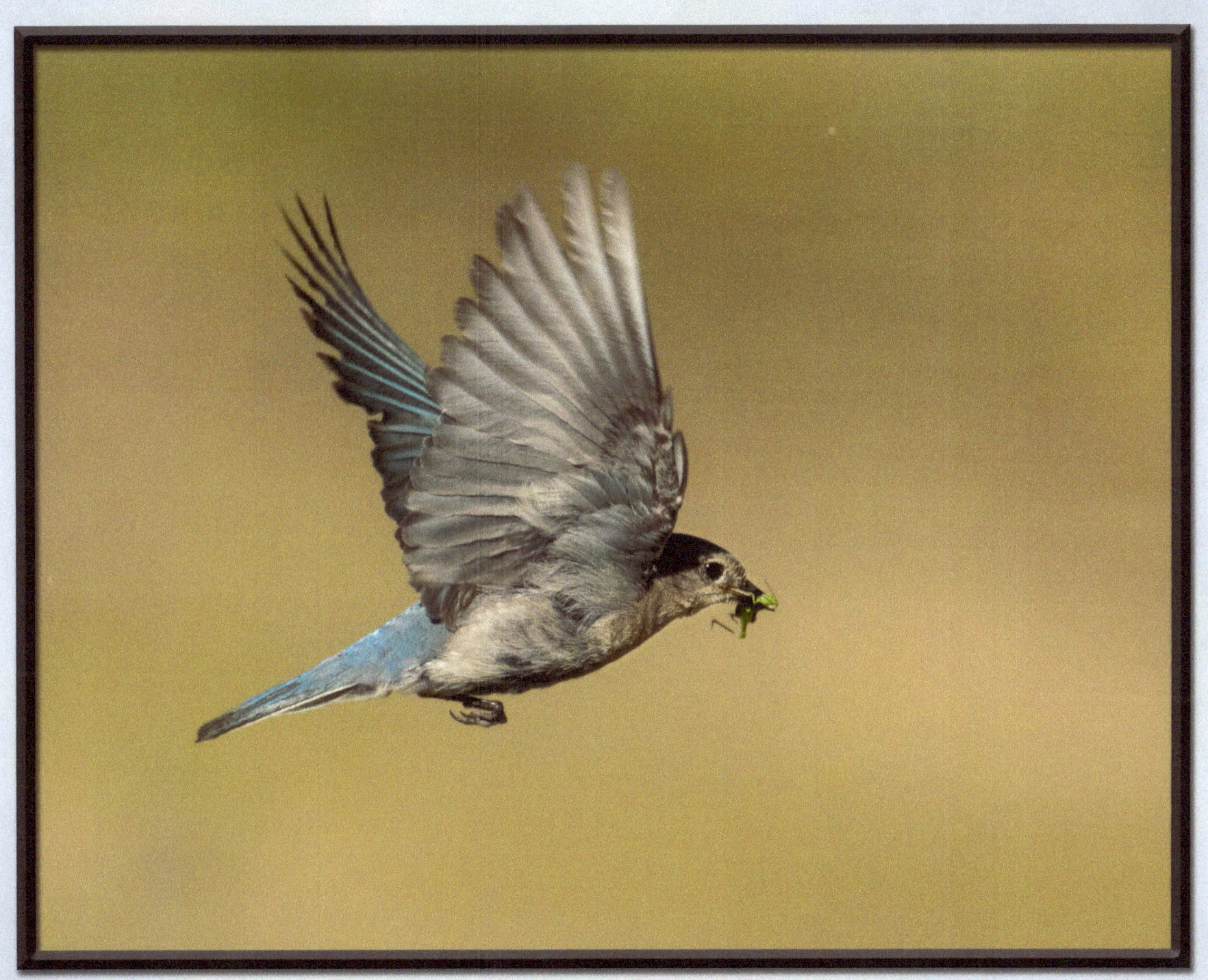

Mama bluebird brings a green grasshopper to the chicks.

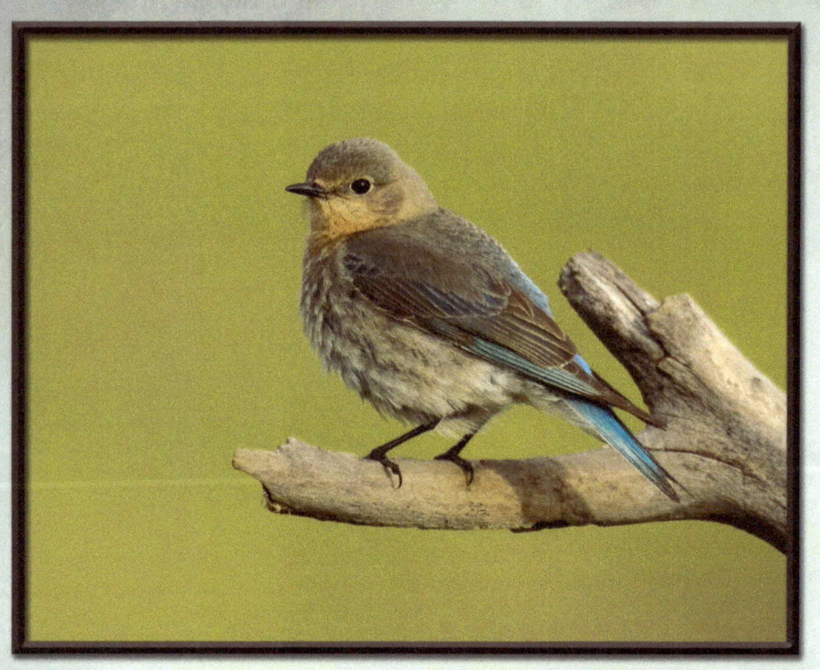

Mama perches
on an old dead
branch to
watch for bugs.

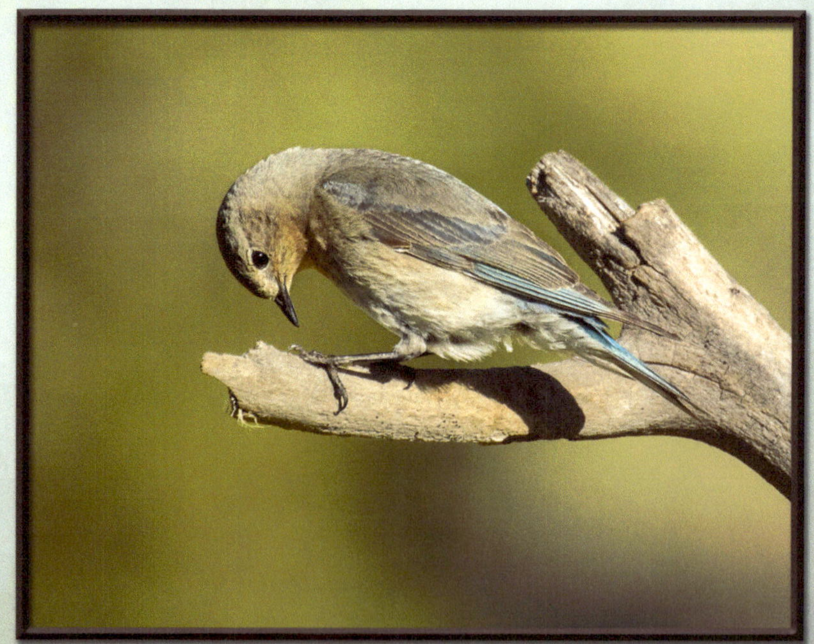

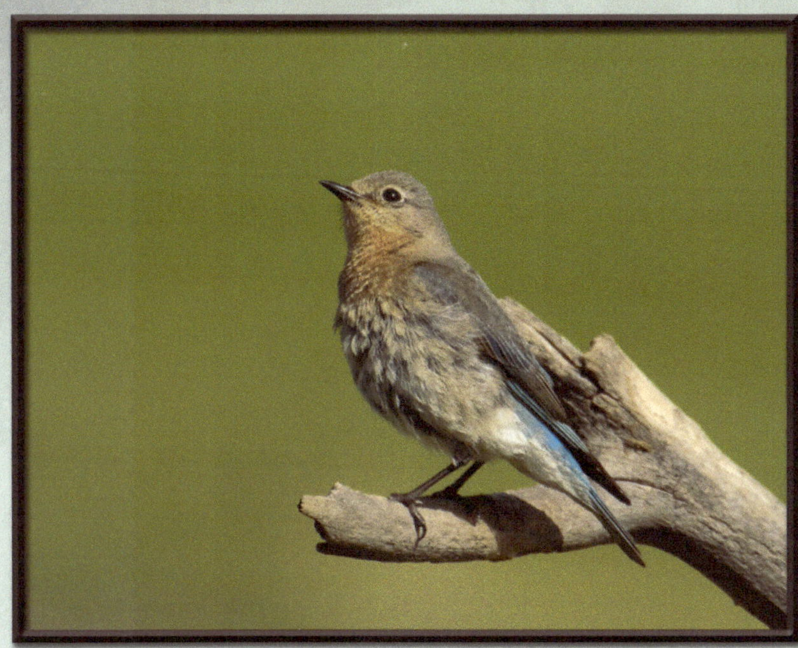

I heard the cry of
a hawk overhead.
Immediately the
bluebirds were at
full attention. Their
soft tweet was
suddenly a little
louder and faster
to teach the babies
the sounds of danger.

While the babies
are growing, the
parents will carry
away the baby's
waste products in
the form of neat
little bundles called
"fecal sacs."

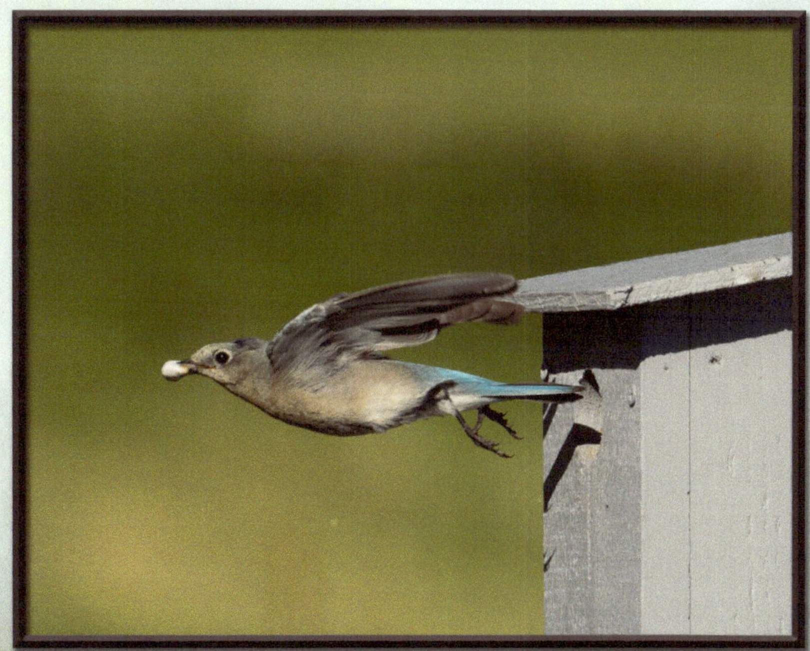

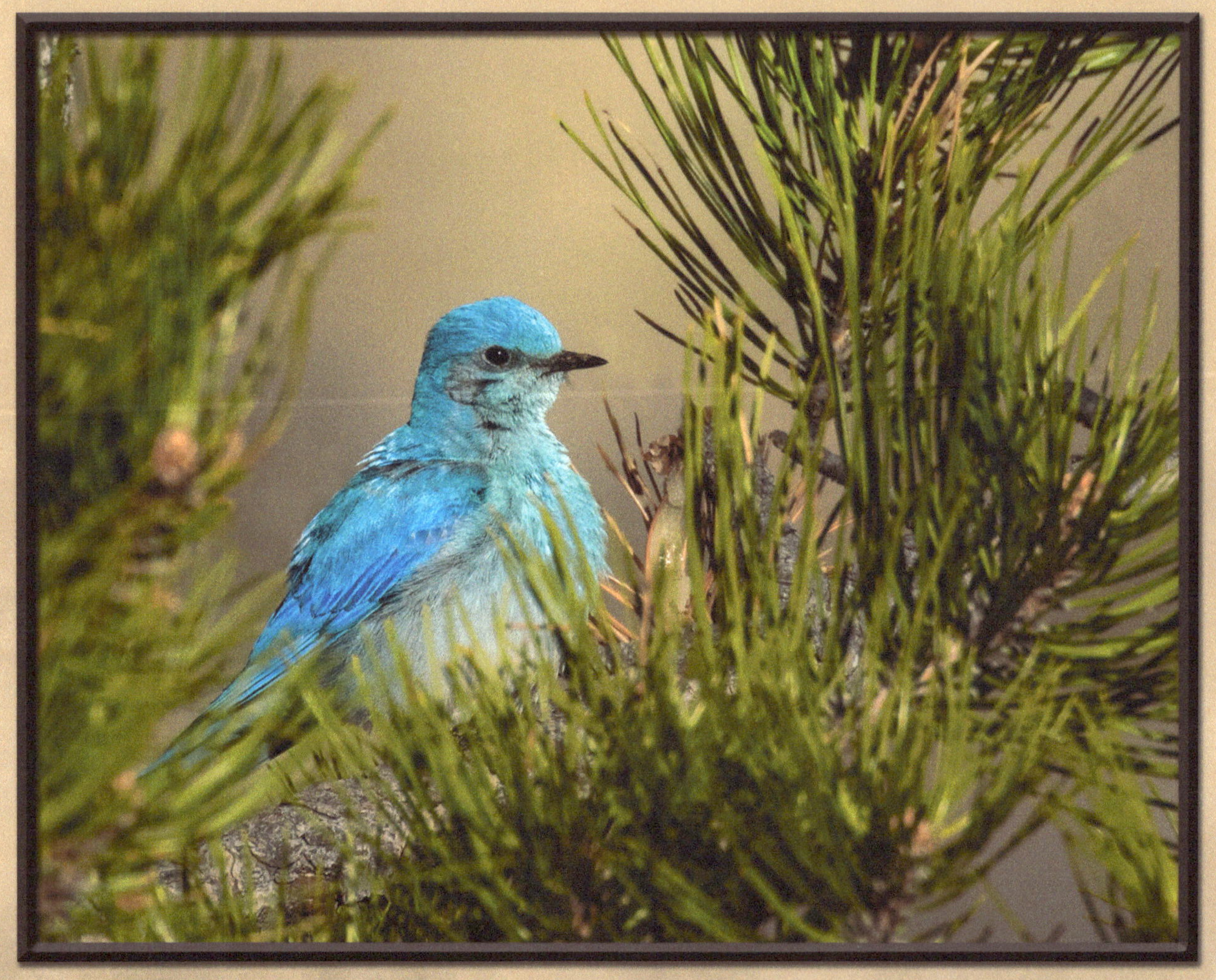

The male would stop and rest in the pine tree for a few minutes between feedings and then he was off hunting for more food.

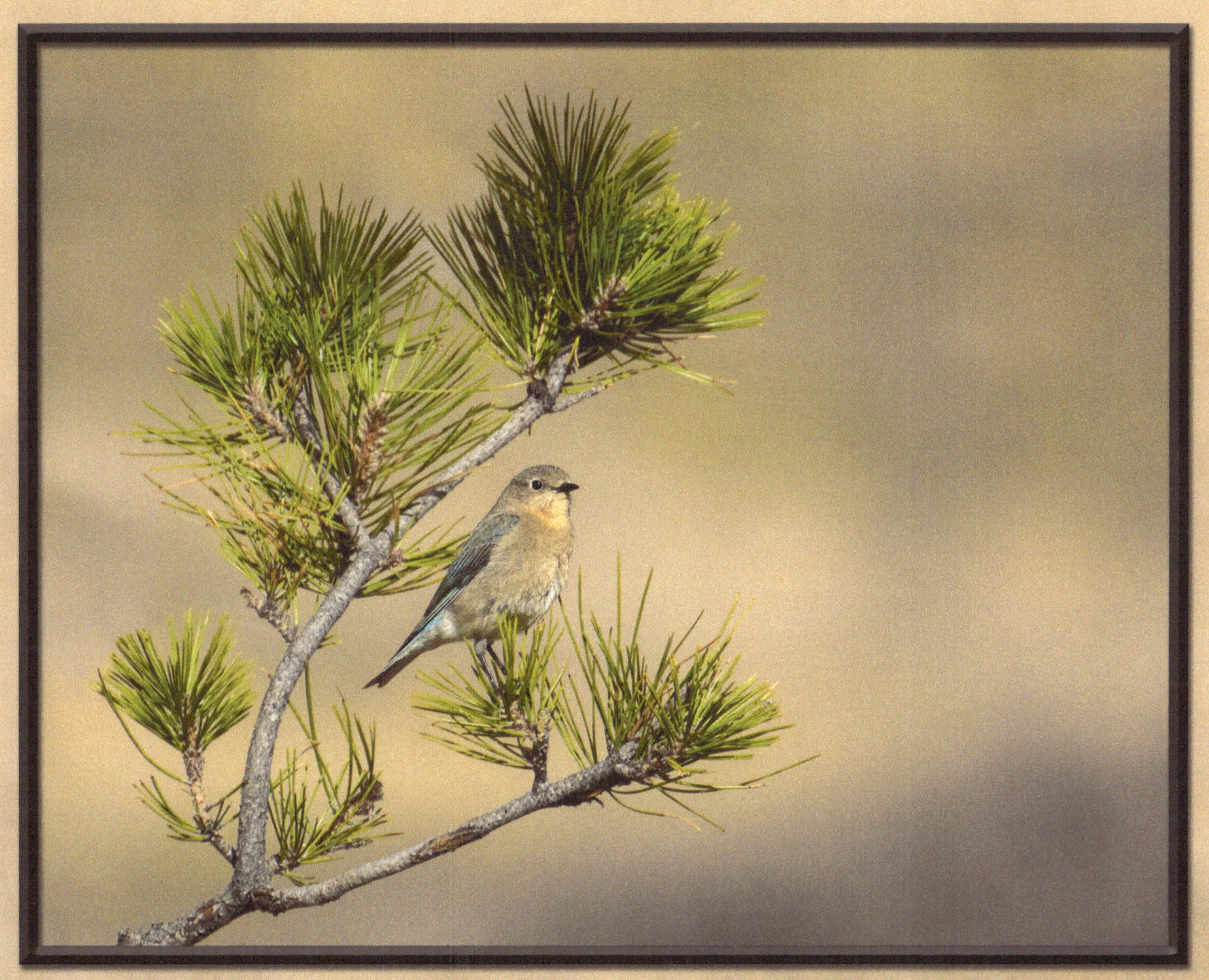

Mama resting in the pine tree between feedings.

At about two weeks
old, the baby's beak
looks disproportionately
large for the body.
The color on their
wings are visible and
they have down
feathers on their
head. The chicks
remain in the nest
for about nineteen
to twenty-two days.

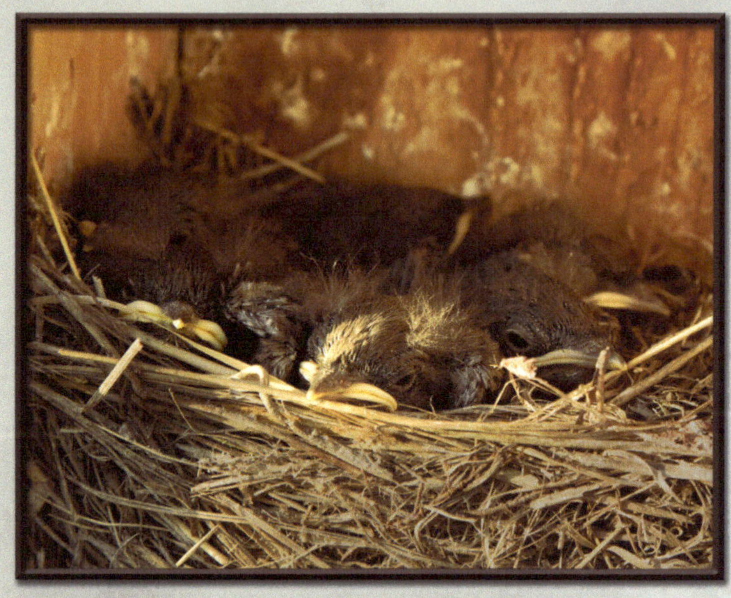

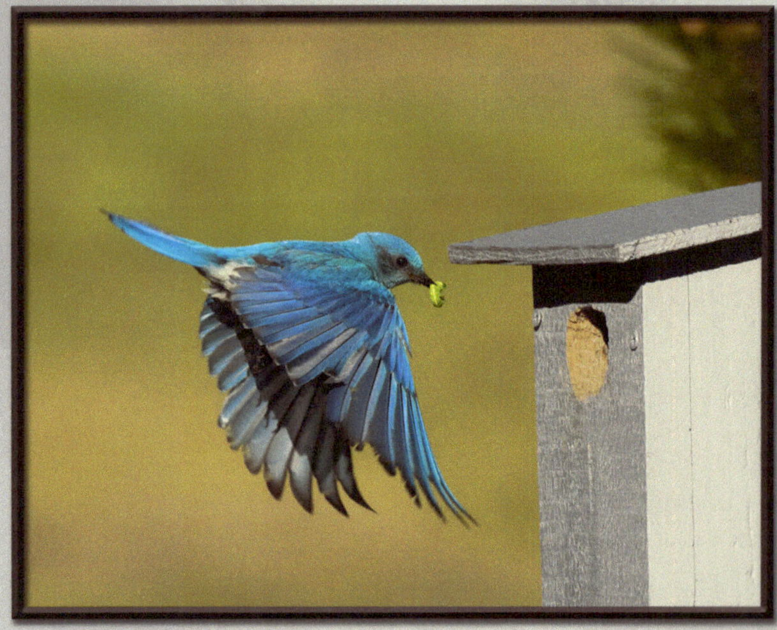

One day I noticed
the Daddy bluebird
bring food to the
nesting box, look
inside and then
leave with the
grasshopper still in
its beak. I thought
that was strange.
Then I noticed him
do it again. Soon
it dawned on me
that he was trying
to lure the chicks
out of the nesting
box. It was time for
them to learn to fly.

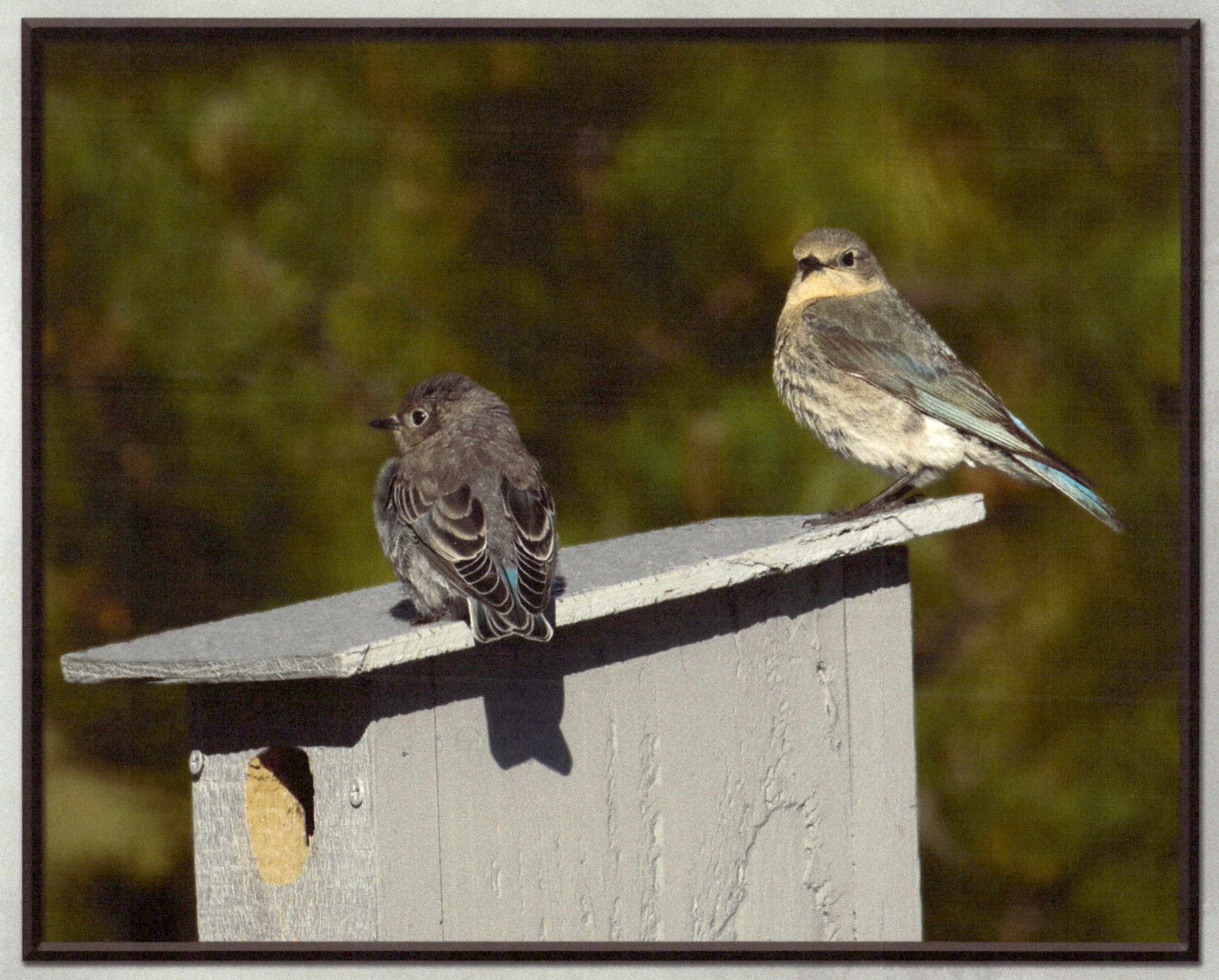

After considerable coaxing the baby bluebirds did come out of the nest, but they did not go far.

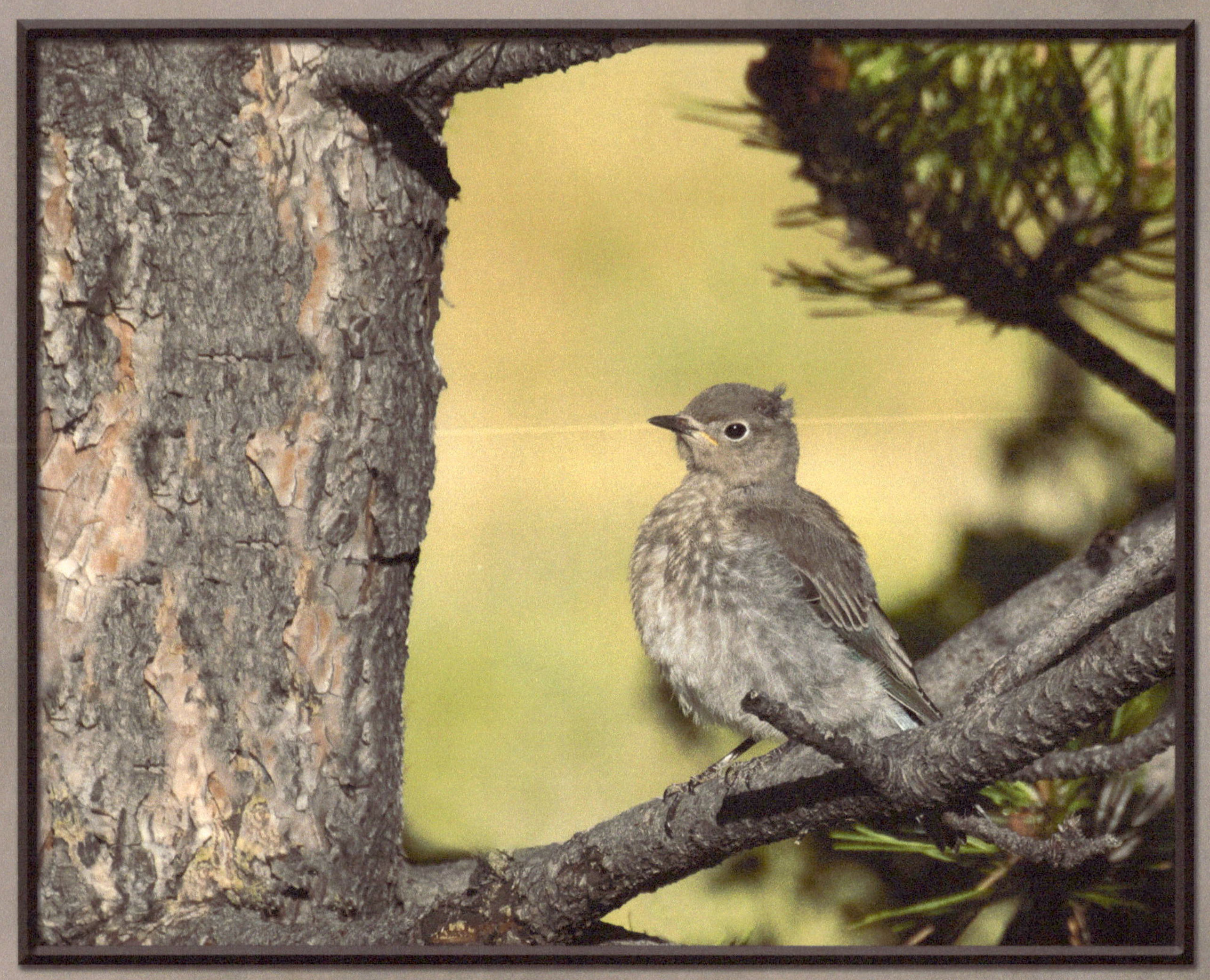

It wasn't long before the baby bluebirds started exploring their new world.

Mama flew
from tree to
tree teaching
them to fly
short distances.

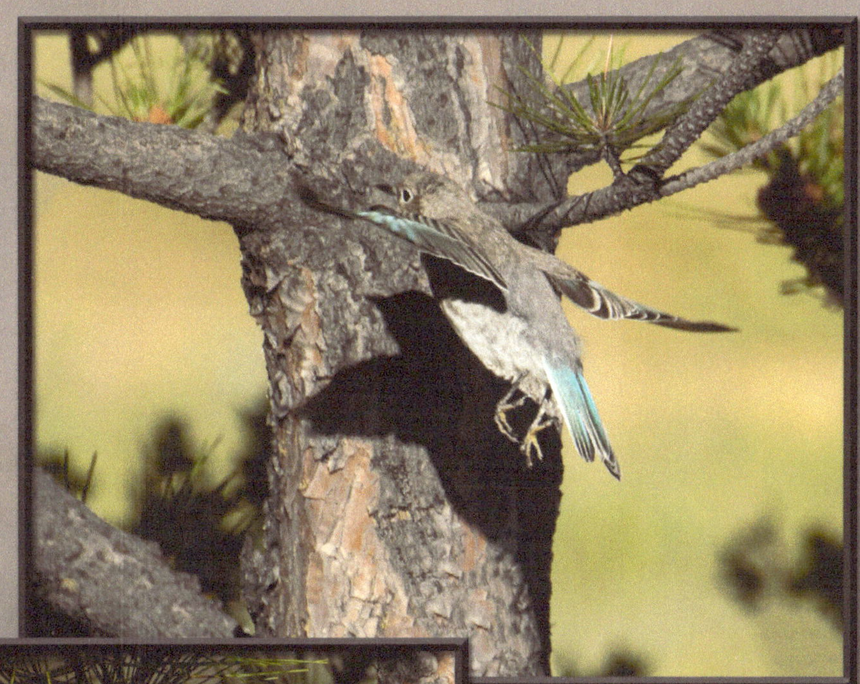

For the first
three days after
they leave the
nest the babies
are still very
dependent on
the parents for
food. The baby
chirped loudly to
tell Mom and
Dad where to
bring the food.

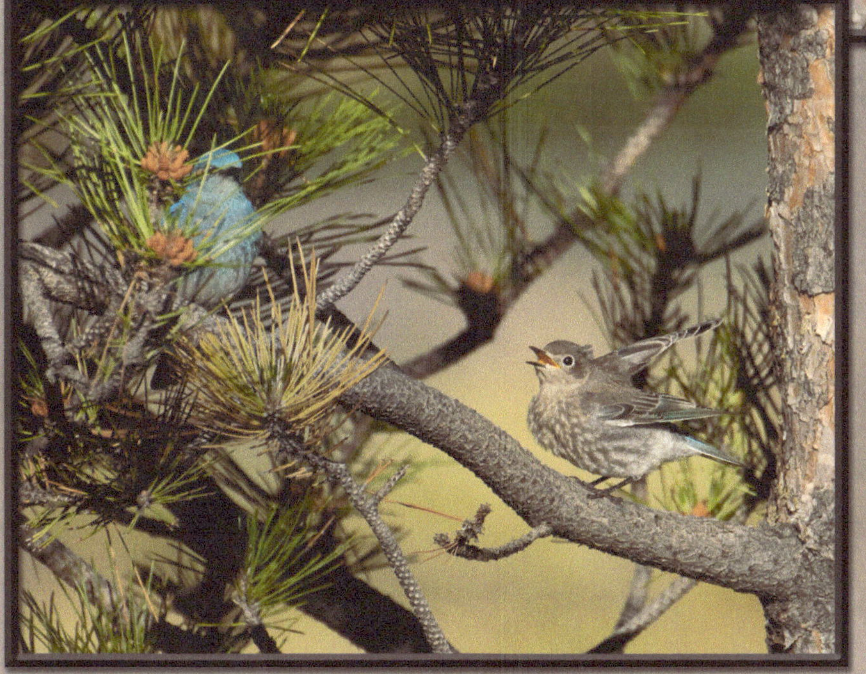

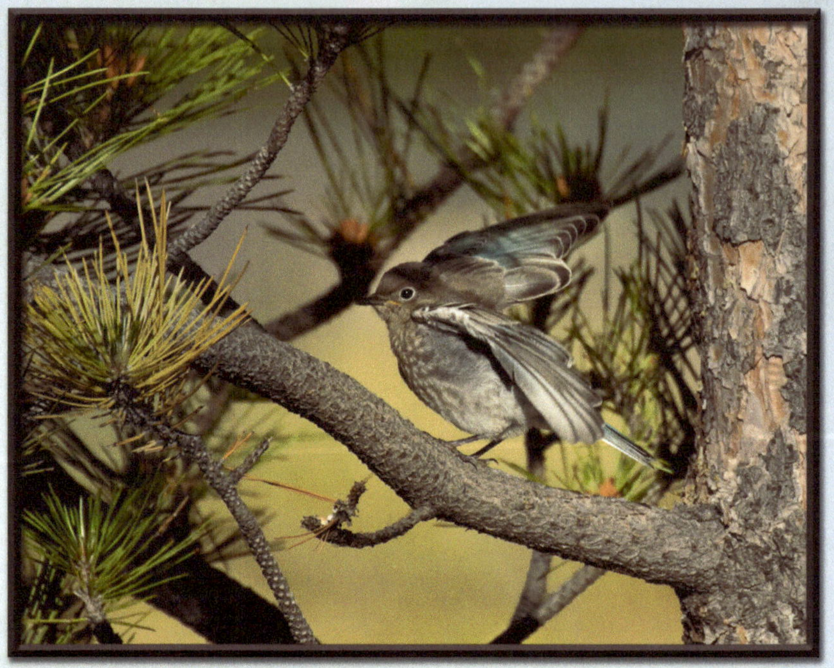

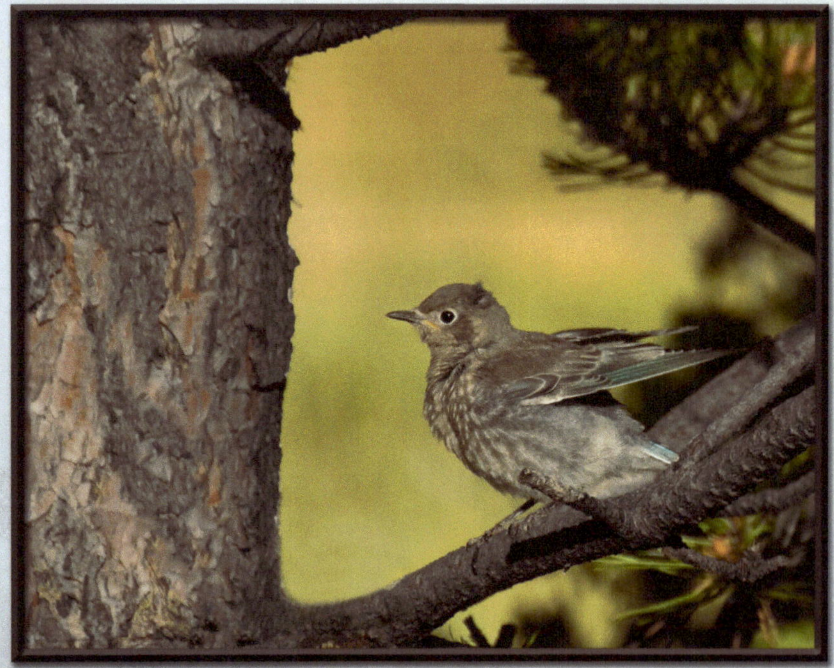

I watched the babies
fly from one side of
the tree trunk to the
other, exercising
their wings and doing
practice flights.

The baby bluebird landed on an old dead branch near the nesting box and watched as Mom and Dad hunted for bugs nearby. By about the tenth day after they fledge the babies are catching their own food.

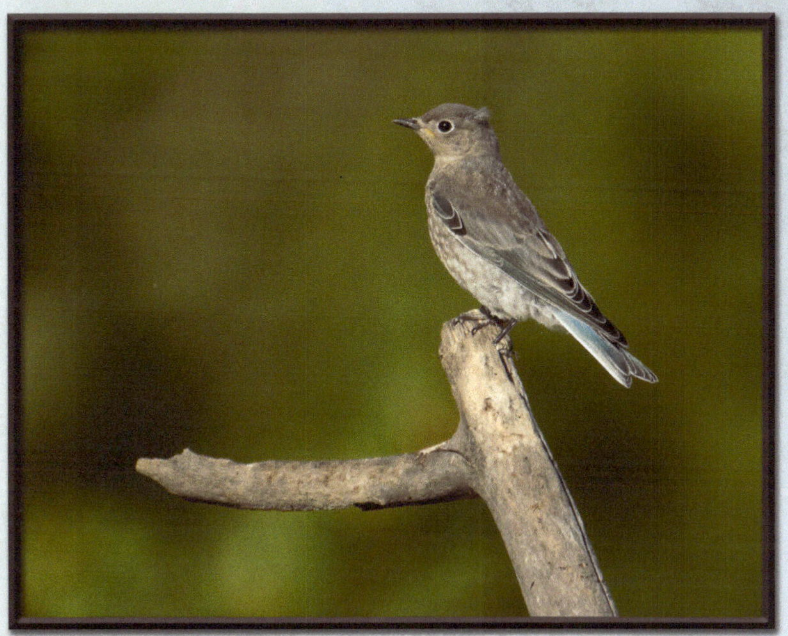

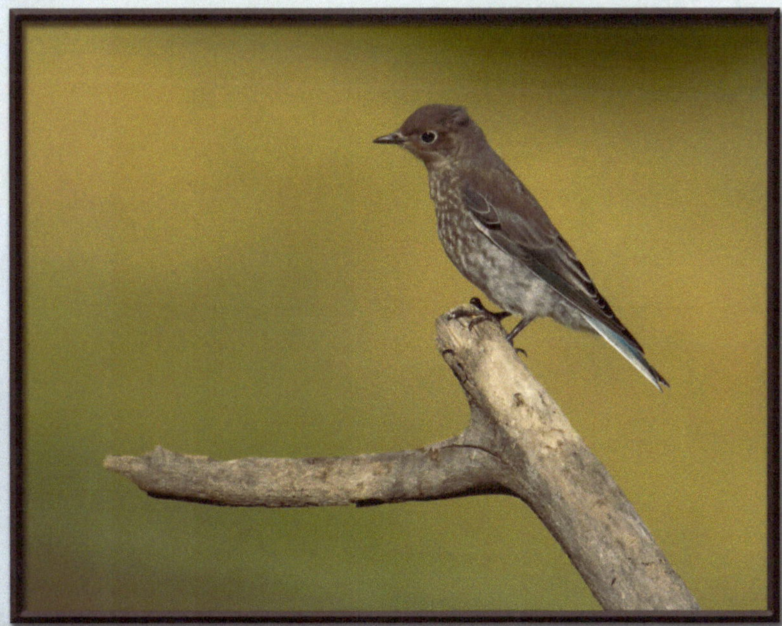

As the baby bluebird watched Mom and Dad hunt, suddenly it saw a movement in the grass. Now if it could just catch that bug.

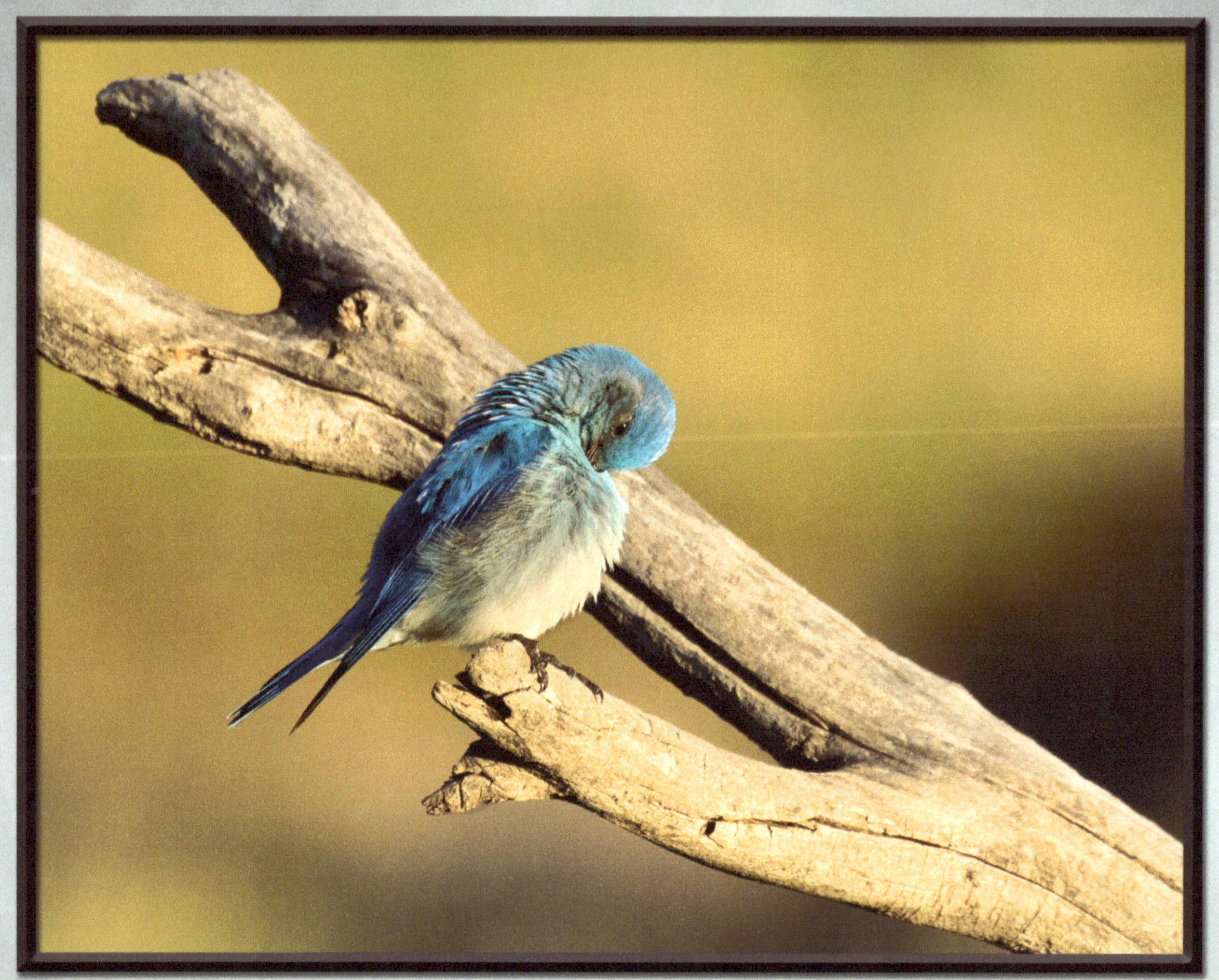

Preening is the bird's way of keeping their feathers in optimum condition. They preen to remove any dust, parasites or food particles that may have gotten on their feathers. Birds have a gland near the base of their tail that produces oil that helps waterproof their feathers and keep them flexible. While preening, birds spread this oil to each feather, so they are evenly coated and protected.

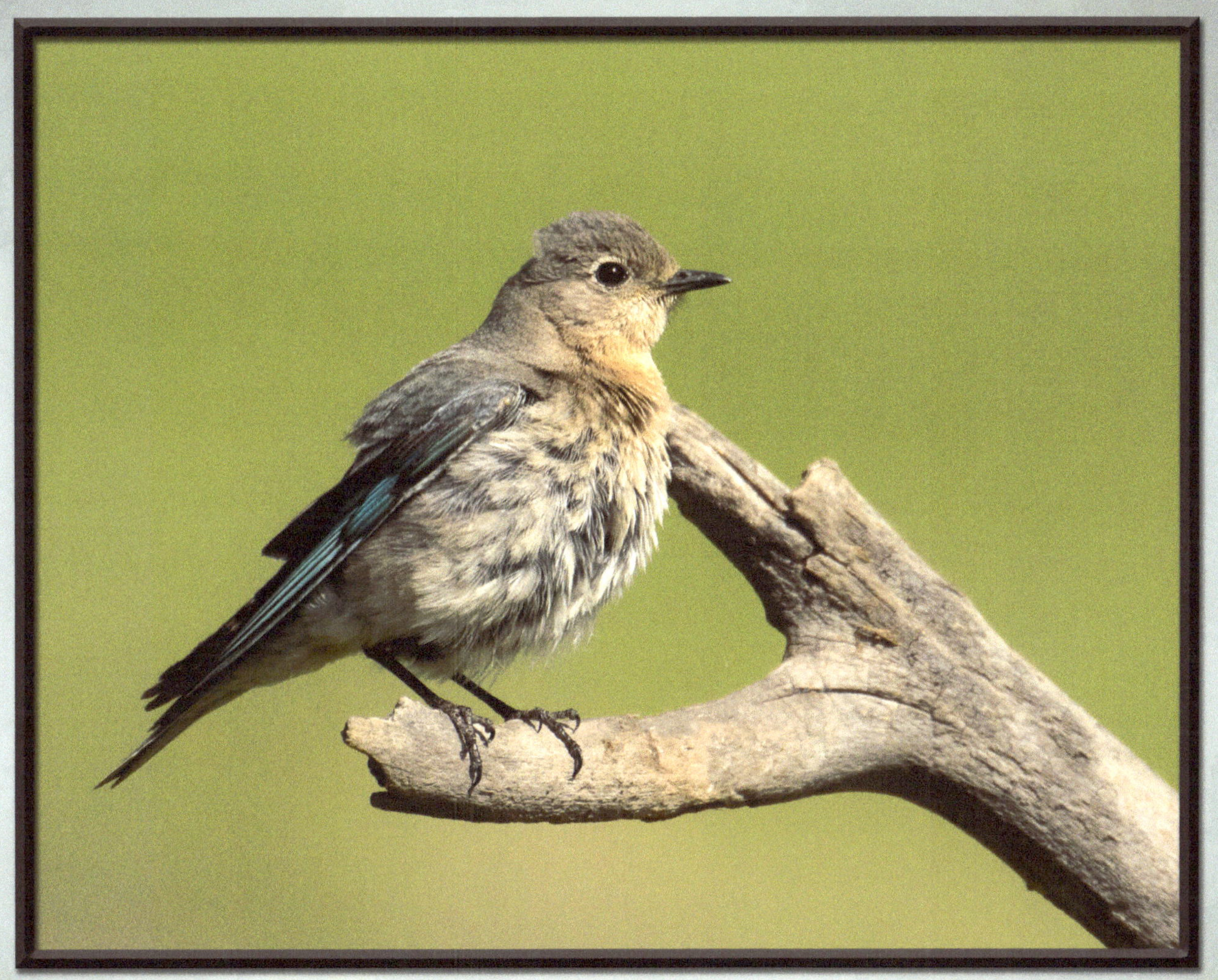

Stretching allows space between the feathers so each feather can be groomed more effectively. Quite often you will see a bird stretch or shake to fluff its feathers after preening.

Birds use their beak
and feet to preen
their feathers and get
them in just the right
position, so they are
waterproofed and
insulated to protect
against extreme hot
or cold temperatures.

Instinctively the babies
knew that they should
preen their feathers.

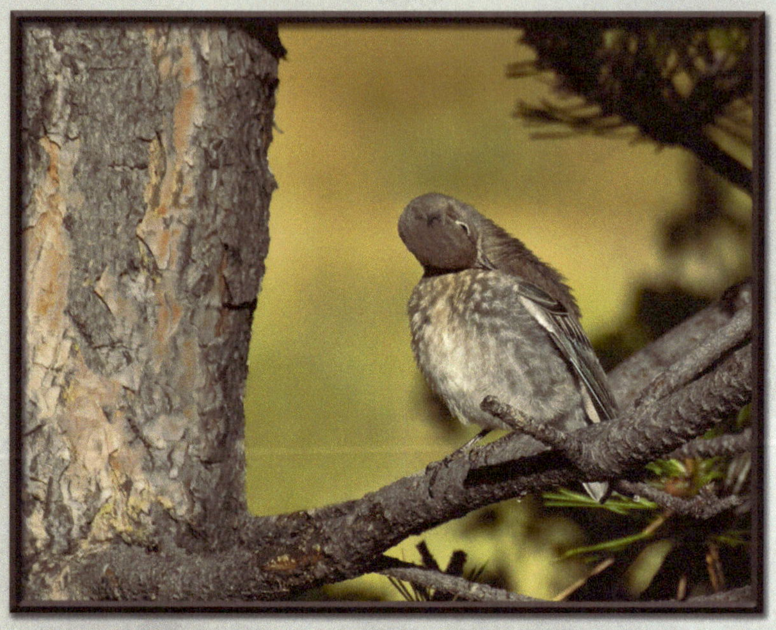

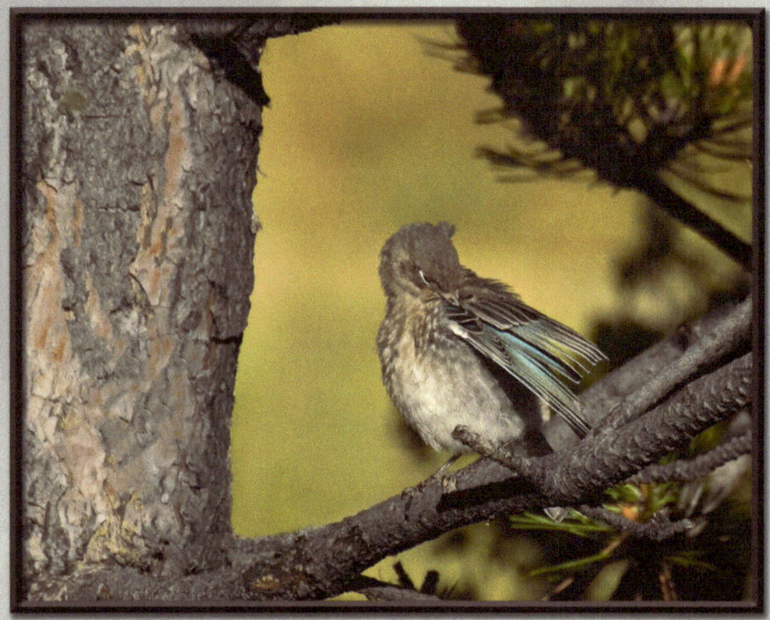

Birds also preen to
align the feathers
into the most
aerodynamic shape
for easier, more
efficient flight.
This helps birds
use less energy
in flight.

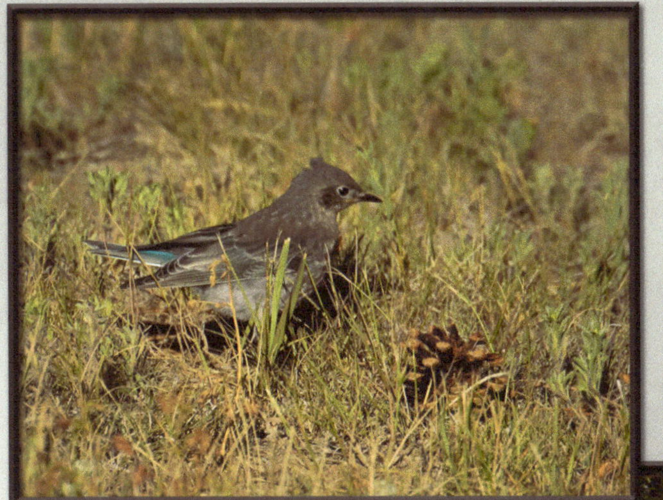

After three to four weeks
the babies are getting pretty
good at finding food.
Following Mom and Dad
from tree to tree and trying
to look for bugs to eat is
a lot of work. The baby was
very tired, so it found a
branch where it could take
a nap.

The days in Colorado get shorter and colder by mid–September.
The mountain bluebird begins to form a flock of thirty or more
birds. Each flock centers on one or more families with the
fledglings and are joined later by other adult birds who failed
to reproduce that year. In late September to early October as
the fledglings become more mobile they migrate to their winter
grounds in the southwestern United States and Mexico leaving
us eagerly awaiting their return next Spring.

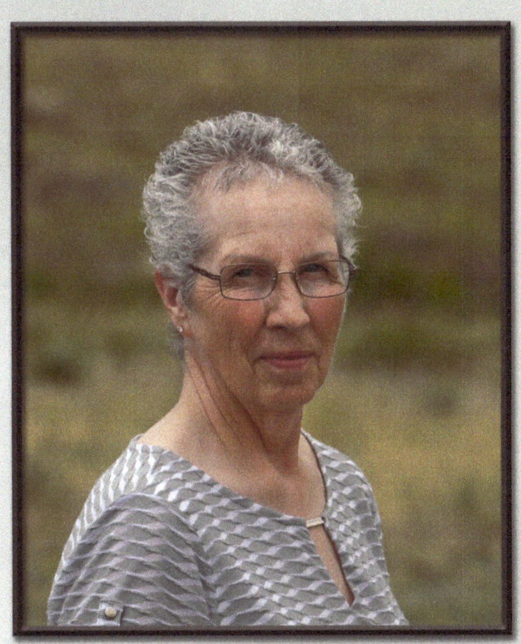

About the Author

Photography is more than taking a picture for Lois. It is a connection with nature; with the beauty that God has created for us to enjoy. Photography causes her to look deeper, be more curious, learn more about her subject and try to bring the viewer on that journey with her.

Sometimes things happen in nature that leave us wondering, "Did I really see what I think I saw?" The high speed of the shutter captures many wonderful and fascinating moments that lead to further research and knowledge.

Lois likes to capture the stormy moods of nature and scenes of what happens in the outdoors. She is fascinated with communication and body language among wildlife and enjoys the challenge of trying to memorialize that connection in a photograph. Lois spends a lot of time studying her subjects to learn their behavior and anticipate their moves so she can capture the precise second of the desired action.